Baseball Signs and Signals

BY TOM PETROFF
WITH JACK CLARY

Photography by Sports Action Photography/Jon Naso

A MOUNTAIN LION AND  MILLER PRESS BOOK

Taylor Publishing Company
Dallas, Texas

BOOK DESIGN BY DILIP KANE, GEORGE WEVER, RICH VITTI
AND BILL PASILIAVICH

Library of Congress Cataloging-in-Publication Data

Petroff, Tom.
  Baseball signs and signals.

  Includes index.
  1. Baseball.   2. Signs and symbols.   I. Clary,
Jack T.   II. Title.
GV867.3.P48   1986   796.357′2   87-489
ISBN 0-87833-545-5

Printed in the United States of America
9   8   7   6   5   4   3   2   1

CONTENTS

ACKNOWLEDGMENTS

Baseball Signs and Signals is literally a sign of a growing phenomenon in book publishing—book producing. Which is simply the creation, development and production of a book by a source *outside* the publishing house. *Baseball Signs and Signals* was produced by Mountain Lion, Inc. and The Miller Press, Inc., two independent book producers that specialize in bringing sports, health and fitness books to market.

In producing this book from concept to mechanicals, the producers brought together and relied on the special skills of many people. The following persons contributed over the past several months to producing *Baseball Signs and Signals,* and to them we say, "Thanks."

- Author/Coach Tom Petroff and writer Jack Clary, who collaborated to set forth a clear and concise text.
- Jeff Torborg, New York Yankee coach and former major league manager, who reviewed the manuscript and penned the introduction.
- Jon Naso of Sports Action Photography, who took nearly all the photographs; Chuck Hartman of Virginia Tech, Dan Shaffer and Chris Dunn of the University of Iowa, who demonstrated Coach Petroff's signs and signals system.
- Bob Frese and Dominique Gioia of Taylor Publishing, who enthusiastically greeted our idea for the book.
- Guy Spencer and Ralph Sparber of Mountain Lion, Inc. and Dave Gibbons of The Miller Press, Inc., who helped edit and proof the manuscript and select the photographs.
- Also, Richard Bresciani of the Boston Red Sox, Jim Ferguson of the Cincinnati Reds, Jay Horowitz of the New York Mets, and Robert W. Brown of the Baltimore Orioles, media relations directors; Dilip Kane of Creative Design Studio, and George Wever, designers; Bill Pasiliavich of Production Graphics; and Richard Vitti and the entire staff of the Elizabeth Typesetting Company.
- And finally, Rust Glover, who gave us the idea.

John J. Monteleone
Mountain Lion, Inc.
Rocky Hill, NJ
October, 1986

Angela Miller
The Miller Press
New York, NY
October, 1986

INTRODUCTION

Although I don't consider myself an "old-timer" in any sense of the word, it seems as though I've been in baseball for most of my life. Like most of my colleagues, I started in the Little League and progressed through the many steps of organized baseball, enjoying the past twenty-three years at the major league level as a player, coach and manager. Throughout my thirty-five plus years in the game, the crucial importance of signs and signals has always been stressed.

The types of communication used at every level of competition are an integral part of our game of baseball. Signs and signals are not only interesting, but they are absolutely necessary. Without them, the individual abilities of the players could not as easily be coordinated into a smooth—and winning—concept of team play. The game itself cannot begin without the catcher's first sign to his pitcher.

A great deal has been written about the mechanics of individual position play in baseball, but there has been very little research or writing about the inside strategies of the game as they relate to giving and receiving signs and signals. Recently I heard that Tom Petroff was writing a book called BASEBALL SIGNS AND SIGNALS. I have known Tom since my college days when I played at Rutgers University against his Rider College teams, and Tom is certainly qualified to write such a book. His years of baseball coaching and administrative experience have resulted in his induction into the College Baseball Coaches Hall of Fame. He is widely respected as one of the most astute coaches at any level of baseball. Tom begins this book with the premise that baseball signs and signals are both informative and fun for players, coaches and fans alike. He has directed the book toward all levels of competition.

Of course, the types of signs and signals that we use with the Yankees tend to be more numerous and complex than those used at the college level, and so on down the ladder to the Little Leagues. At the higher levels of the game—and particularly in the major leagues—teams are constantly attempting to steal their opponents' signs so they can gain an advantage by predicting the opponents' next play or pitch. I was managing the Cleveland Indians some years ago when I realized that one of our TV commentators had learned our signs from one of our players and was amazing his audience with his expertise by predicting what we would do in every situation. Unfortunately, our opponents became wise to our system while watching TV in their clubhouse and quickly used their own system of signals to their hitters and pitchers to combat our strategy.

The whole intrigue of signs and signals can become very mysterious—as well as comical, at times, depending on the proficiency of the sign-givers and sign-takers. Nothing looks worse in a ballgame than a pitcher making a pitch and the catcher never laying a glove on it...or a strike that carries all the way to the backstop on the fly because pitcher and catcher crossed up their signs...or a baserunner breaking for the plate on what he thought was a squeeze play and the hitter who missed the sign standing there wondering what this nut is trying to do by coming way down the third-base line. I have seen these gaffes occur at all levels of baseball.

BASEBALL SIGNS AND SIGNALS will help fans garner inside information on the whole "myster" of signs and signals so they can be a step ahead of the game and impress all of their peers with their great knowledge of baseball. It will help coaches and players at every level establish and implement their systems of signs and signals effectively, which will benefit the overall quality of their play enormously.

The importance of signs and signals to the game of baseball cannot be understated. I would urge anyone who wants to understand the game thoroughly and/or to play it well to study this book; it answers the questions that players, coaches and fans have about signs and is a highly useful addition to any baseball-minded person's library.

—Jeff Torborg, Coach
New York Yankees

CHAPTER 1

BASEBALL SIGNS: THE SECRET LANGUAGE

Like any great American institution, baseball has its own brand of communication. The players have their own jargon— "bringing the heat" is throwing a fastball...putting a pitch in a batter's "wheelhouse" is throwing it right where he likes it—but unique to the sport is the great variety of its unspoken language. In no other sport can players do so much on the field by saying so little—or sometimes nothing at all.

Certainly, anyone who has attended baseball games at levels higher than youth leagues, and particularly at a major league level, has marveled at the gyrations and motions that third base coaches employ as they send strategies to batters and base runners. Everyone knows that pitcher and catcher communicate with each other before every pitch by a series of finger and hand signals, and that infielders relay information back and forth with gloves shielding their mouths though they may say not a word. Managers move players all over a field with an arm movement or the wave of a towel; they send for relief pitchers with a touch of a right or left arm; and they operate a communications network to and from the dugout or bench to their coaches that rivals any espionage network.

Coaches at first and third base direct traffic with a wave of an arm or a thrust of a fist as if they were policemen at a busy intersection, every body movement necessary to keep traffic going...and, sometimes more importantly, not going. Often fans are so caught up in the game as it unfolds around these coaches that they rarely see all of the player action. As a result, coaches work in relative obscurity—unless, of course, they send a runner home and the man is thrown out at the plate.

Baseball's unspoken language has been a part of the game for nearly a century. The original Baltimore Orioles of the National League, with such players as John McGraw, Hughey Jennings, Wilbert Robinson, and Wee Willie Keeler, devised the first bits of truly "inside baseball" strategy. This group first perfected such maneuvers as the bunt, the hit-and-run play, the squeeze, and the double steal. Most baseball historians credit a man named Ned Hanlon, who managed those Baltimore teams in the late 1890s, as the creator. The plays he conceived and taught his team to execute left the rest of his league reeling, because baseball, as then played, was basically a pitch-hit-catch game.

In fact, the story is told of how the Orioles executed thirteen hit-and-run plays in sweeping a four-game series against the New York Giants. The Giants manager, John Ward, threatened to haul Hanlon before the league's commissioner "because he wasn't playing baseball; it was some new game that he invented." Even after teams copied Hanlon's plays, he devised ways to stop them.

McGraw, Jennings, and Robinson later became great managers in the major leagues early in the twentieth century. The things they had learned as players in Baltimore soon became commonplace with their team, and hence throughout all of organized baseball. Today, we see the end result of that guile in the unspoken language that we will discuss throughout this book.

Cap That!

The late Jack Coombs, one of college baseball's greatest coaches who also had a superlative pitching career in the major leagues with the Philadelphia Athletics and Brooklyn Dodgers, gave sage advice on the vagaries of giving signs and signals:

"I once requested my freshman coach to use a very simple set of signals that could be given by some player on his [Duke] squad—some player who was not actively in the game.

"This young coach decided that a red-haired boy would be the proper fellow to flash the signals because he was very easy to see. The coach decided the redhead should take off his cap for the steal signal. His cap held in his left hand was the sign for the hit-and-run play. These were very conspicuous signs, very simple and very easily seen by everyone on the team.

"With the score tied 2-2 in the sixth inning, I suddenly witnessed some of the most unorthodox baseball I ever had seen from an offensive standpoint. The first batter took first base when hit by a pitch, and then stole second, third, and home on the next three pitches.

"The next batter singled, and then stole second and third on the next two pitches. He scored when the batter hit a sacrifice fly on the third pitch.

TO HIT OR NOT TO HIT: GIVING SIGNS TO THE BATTER

The most intricate system of signs and signals in baseball is that which takes place between the batter and the baseline coaches, particularly the third base coach. With runners on base, signals are flashed on nearly every pitch to dictate the strategy the coach wishes to use. It is up to the batter and the base runner to recognize these signs and execute them.

It also is up to the manager or head coach to establish his system, or a package of signs, by utilizing one basic philosophy: simplicity. The best system in the world is no good unless it works. The best way to insure that is to install a system that is understood by every member of the team, is successful when used, and cannot easily be detected by the opposition.

Simplicity, of course, is a relative term in setting up such a package. The higher the level of baseball competition, the fewer signs are used. In the major leagues, for example, most teams have only four or five basic signs between coach and batter: hit-and-run, take the pitch, squeeze bunt, steal, and sacrifice. But such is the skill level in the major leagues that players are able to do other phases of the offensive game on their own.

On the other hand, I've known some amateur teams that have as many as nine or ten signs, covering nearly anything that can happen to a batter or runner during a turn at bat. I believe that too many signs can be worse than too few because, again depending on the level of competition, a player's mind and concentration can be muddled if he must try to sort through a maze of different signals.

It also can muddle a coach's thinking. Walter Alston, the late, great manager of the Dodgers, always believed that a simple, effective means of communication gave him more latitude in coordinating all of the individual efforts into team success. So he was very precise in devising a system that did not take too much mental effort to understand, even among major league players who had total familiarity with this kind of communication.

I believe that if this philosophy is sound enough for accomplished professionals, it certainly makes sense for those competing at much lower levels. And my own experience in coaching on three major collegiate levels of competition, as well as on the international level, has proved to me the efficacy of this position.

The most common signs given by a coach number as many as six: flash signals, combination signals, count signals, word signals, holding signals, and block signals. We will concentrate on the latter two, the holding and block signals, because I believe they are best for other than the higher levels of competition. We will discuss them in detail in a moment after a quick look at the others:

1. **Flash Signals:** These are quick touches by a coach along some part of his body, "flashed" so they cannot be easily detected. They begin with an indicator, yet the quickness also is a drawback in lower levels of competition because players may not be adept at reading this rapid-fire series of signs, which really are no more than a quick touch of the hand or a flick of a finger.

2. **Combination Signals:** These are two or more motions given together that represent a single sign. For instance, a touch of a cap and one at the jersey's letters mean nothing unless given together. One of them is the key sign, but it must follow or precede the other. If there is an interruption or touching of some other part of the body and uniform between them, there is no sign.

3. **Count Signals:** A coach's torso is divided up into sections and each is given a numerical quantity, beginning with one and extending to how many parts have been determined. Signs such as bunt, hit-and-run, steal, etc., are given numerical totals (bunt = 2; hit-and-run = 4; steal = 5) and the batter and runner must add the number of touches to each area to get the sign. The coach delivers a stop sign, such as clapping hands, to indicate the touches are completed. You can see how young players might miss a sign or become confused with that system.

4. **Word Signs:** Just what it signifies—a word, or verbal command, is used to point to a certain sign. Often these are used just for squeeze plays where the action will be instantaneous. For instance, a third base coach can yell to the batter—so loud the runner at third will also hear him—"Let's get a good pitch." The word "pitch," when uttered by the coach with a man on third, alerts the batter that something is coming, and then he must look for the sign to lay down a squeeze bunt. Of course, crowd noise can be a drawback to any extensive use of verbal signs.

Now, let's concentrate on the other two packages, the *holding system* and the *blocking system*.

HOLDING SYSTEM: As the term implies, holding signals are those that are stopped or held for extra time so the batter and runner can read them. These are ideal for younger players who are learning how to get information from a coach by hand signals. In giving them, a coach can go through his motions and when he gets to the sign for the strategy to be used— the "hot sign," some call it—then he will maintain his hand, fist, or finger at that spot for perhaps a couple of seconds so the player cannot miss it. He can even look more than once if he has any doubts.

"Then came two out, and the fifth batter was safe at first on an error. On the next two pitches, he stole second and third base. I couldn't stand it any longer, and I rushed from my seat in the stands to the bench to find out why such offensive tactics were being employed. The answer came quickly: That red-haired boy had taken off his cap and forgot to put it back on his head.

"From that day on, I never asked any of my players to take the responsibility for giving the offensive signals. An older man is free from that mental attitude which often causes a younger person to forget himself."

Gathering Information

There are thirteen basic factors that a coach must consider when he makes strategic decisions, and before he flashes a sign for both offensive and defensive situations:

(1) Whether the team is home or away
(2) The score
(3) The inning
(4) The situation with outs and men on base
(5) Upcoming hitters and skills of each
(6) Baserunning skills of men on base and upcoming hitters for each particular situation
(7) Bench players available for pinch-hitting and pinch-running
(8) Your pitcher's fatigue factor
(9) Your bullpen strength
(10) Opposing pitcher's fatigue and control
(11) Opposition's bullpen strength
(12) Opposition's fielding skills on special plays
(13) Throwing strength and accuracy of opposition's outfielders and infielders on potential relay plays

I believe it is best to give these signals by either facing the batter directly or walking toward him—all the while giving the batter a full body view so as to get his absolute attention.

The drawback to this package is that the sign can be stolen by the opposition because of its obvious nature. However, a coach can lessen this danger by maintaining a rhythm that is not obviously interrupted when he gives a particular sign; by preceding and following the sign with other signals that mean nothing, he also can add a nuance to the sign itself. For instance, a clenched fist with the thumb extended might be the sign for a bunt. But a clenched fist without the thumb would mean nothing at all. In giving the sign, the coach would "hold" the fist clenched, without showing his thumb for a couple of seconds so the batter can see there is no sign. Then he can give a few more movements and come back and clench his fist again, this time extending the thumb to alert the batter that he is to bunt, and then continue with other false motions.

BLOCK SYSTEM: This is achieved by dividing the body into sections, such as we have illustrated (Fig. I). As you can see, each section of the body indicates a distinct piece of strategy; this can be translated to the batter and

FLASH SIGNALS

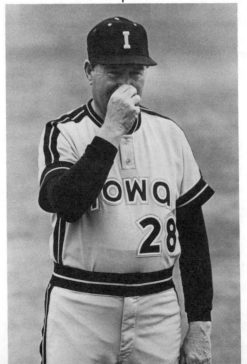

runner by having one side of the body for hitting signals, the other side for the runner's signals.

In using this package, the coach can designate one section of the body for the first three hitters, a second section for the next three, and a third section for the last three. For instance, a hit-and-run could be indicated by touching the upper part of the body for the first three hitters, it could be indicated by touching the letters of the jersey for the second three, and by tapping the belt buckle for the last three, with the sign being determined by a number of rubs to each section of the body.

If two rubs meant hit-and-run, and the coach did that sign on his belt for the second hitter in the batting order, he would ignore it because that is the hit-and-run sign for the last three men in the order. However, if he rubbed the letter on the front of his jersey twice for the fifth hitter with a man on first base, then both would know the hit-and-run would be in effect on the next pitch.

If there is a drawback, it can be for the coach who must keep in mind at all times which hitter is at bat. This system can become tricky in the middle and late innings, particularly if there have been pinch-hitters and his original lineup has been altered. Also, the batter must always keep in mind his numerical position in the batting order, regardless of the inning or whether he has been a mid-game replacement.

COMBINATION SIGNALS

A variation of the block system is one where each square on the block represents an offensive maneuver. This, I believe, is much better used in lower levels of competition because it is very difficult for young players to pick up the relative complications of the traditional block system with its revolving responsibilities. Also, upper levels of competition usually have only four signs—hit-and-run, steal, bunt, and take—so it is much easier to understand the options. In a lower level, where a team's strategy often is governed by its talent, some of those signs could not be used, and others would have to be substituted.

SETTING UP THE SYSTEM

Once the coach decides which package will be used, he must then be certain that it is easily understood and executed by the team. The first part of this procedure is to establish a system for giving the signs. This is a procedure that can have as few as three steps or as many as six. Let's take what I call the "long form" first because the other is simply an offshoot, and each can be used at any point in a game.

COUNT SIGNALS

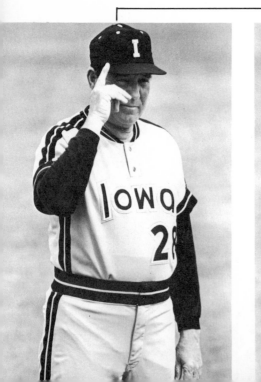

1. **Alert:** This will be a signal to the batter and runner that a sign is coming, and they should now be alert to the sequence that will follow. I favor this for the lower levels of competition because it gets the player's attention. I've always made it a point to allow a hitter to do just that—hit—unless I signal him otherwise; so I may go through a variety of motions but, unless he sees me give a sign that tells him that I soon will want him to do something, he disregards what he sees and hits away.

2. **Indicator:** This is the switch that turns on a particular strategy. A coach may, for example, designate the belt buckle to be the indicator and then decree that the second touch after that will be the hot sign. Until the batter and runner see that indicator, everything before means nothing, unless we utilize the alert system.

Of course, coaches always are on guard for evidence that their indicator sign has been stolen by the opposition. To combat that possibility, a coach also can have a sign that changes the sequence between the indicator and the "hot sign." In the example I gave above, that sign could tell the team that the "hot sign" would become the first touch after the indicator instead of the second touch. To be certain that everyone gets the message, the coach also should verbally alert his players that the switch may be coming.

HOLDING SIGNALS

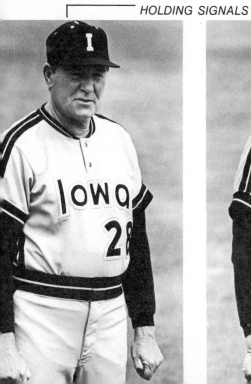
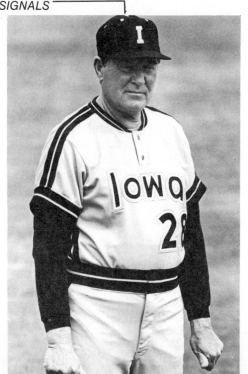

3. **Actual Sign,** or "hot sign," as we've called it, is the motion that tells the batter and runner what must be done on the next pitch, and it should quickly—within one to three moves—follow the indicator. The coach may then continue through another series of motions, all of which will mean nothing because he has given the sign and will not come back to touch either the indicator or hot sign spot unless the batter asks for a repeat. We will discuss the repeat sign later in this chapter.

It is important to stress that once the hot sign has been given, the batter and runner should continue to watch the coach as he goes through his other motions so as not to tip off the opposition to the real sign. This must be stressed at every practice and at every meeting where these signs are discussed. The coach must take precautions that, unless he is using the holding system, *he should make certain all of his gestures and touches are given in a steady, continuous motion even after the sign has been given.* As we will discuss later in the book, there often are eagle-eyed spies sitting on the opposite bench who study every move made by a coach, batter, and runner to try to get the slightest tipoff as to the real sign.

4. **Activator:** This can be used for a valid sign to become truly valid, a stamp of approval on the real sign that just has been given. It can be from a touch, or a hand clap, or even from a coach's stance in the third base coaching box. But whatever it is, the batter must see it to know that the sign he just has received is valid. If this is not given, the sign doesn't mean anything.

5. **Release:** This is a sign by the coach that nothing else is coming and that the batter and runner can look away after a moment or two. This always is given several motions after the hot sign has been flashed, and is a particularly good tool for the young player who will learn to look away at the proper interval following his getting the sign.

6. **Rub-Off:** This erases the hot sign if there has been a sudden change of mind by the coach that may be dictated by second thoughts, or by a sudden shift by the opposition's players. Or, like the activator, it can be used as a bit of counter-espionage if a coach believes his signs have been stolen. He can flash the sign then, either by ignoring the activator or by using the rub-off, negate it, and see if the opposition reacts to the original sign.

As I said earlier, any combination of the above six steps can be used, and at any time during a game. For young players, I believe it is good training for them to be keyed in to the long form because it trains them to look, recognize, follow-through with eye contact, and then execute.

SIMPLIFIED OFFENSIVE PACKAGE

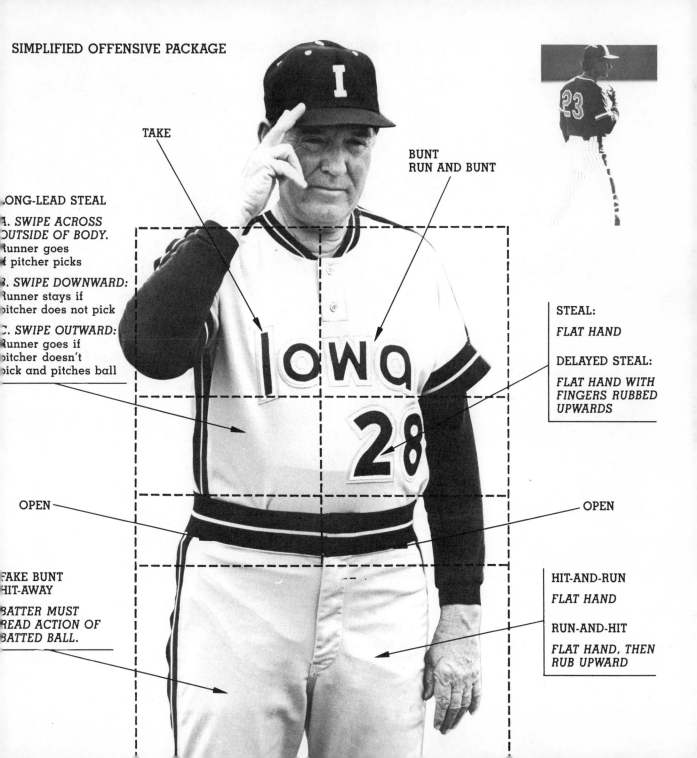

TAKE

BUNT
RUN AND BUNT

LONG-LEAD STEAL

A. SWIPE ACROSS
OUTSIDE OF BODY.
Runner goes
if pitcher picks

B. SWIPE DOWNWARD:
Runner stays if
pitcher does not pick

C. SWIPE OUTWARD:
Runner goes if
pitcher doesn't
pick and pitches ball

STEAL:

FLAT HAND

DELAYED STEAL:

FLAT HAND WITH
FINGERS RUBBED
UPWARDS

OPEN

OPEN

FAKE BUNT
HIT-AWAY

BATTER MUST
READ ACTION OF
BATTED BALL.

HIT-AND-RUN
FLAT HAND

RUN-AND-HIT
FLAT HAND, THEN
RUB UPWARD

Q's to Consider

A baseball coach's decisions in flashing his array of signs and signals can only be as effective as the information he has to help him make those decisions.

Here is what major league super scout Jim Russo looks for:

"What can we expect from the pitcher? Does he follow a pitching pattern? What pitch does he throw to start off a batter? Does he throw breaking stuff on 3-and-2? Does he have a trick pitch, like a forkball or knuckleball? How is he at holding runners on base?"

And for hitters:

"How do we get the man out? Is he a low-ball or high-ball hitter? Does he like the ball in or out? Is he a cripple hitter who gets the go-ahead on 3-and-0? Is he strictly a pull hitter or does he hit to all fields? What is his speed as a base runner, and is he aggressive in taking the extra base?"

PUTTING THE SYSTEM TOGETHER

Sign packages should be installed as quickly as possible after practices have begun. A coach begins by working on techniques and assessing the full capabilities of his players so he will know what kind of team he will have during that season—strong hitters and power or a team that might have to rely on speed and guile with prolific use of hit-and-runs, bunts, squeezes, and aggressiveness on the base paths. All of this will determine basic strategy and I always want my players working on their strong points as soon as possible. This means also working with the various modes we will use with men on base—we incorporate them right into the start of our drills and practice sessions.

To do it right, I believe in a very fundamental approach often beginning with just two signs—for instance, the indicator and the bunt sign. At lower levels, I've used three, beginning with the *alert,* then the *indicator* and *hot sign.* I want the players to get used to seeing them and, once they know their meaning, to actually execute that particular maneuver. It is very helpful to couple this on-the-field action with quizzes away from the field by flashing the signs and then asking the player what his action will be.

Another sign or two is added a couple of days later, and maybe a third the day after that. The sequence will be the same, except that after three signs, the team should go back and review the first one. The add-and-review process is very effective and, once everything has been included, the review process becomes never-ending, because deep in the season players become so used to a system that they get mentally lazy. Periodic reviews are the best method of preventing breakdowns by keeping everyone alert and in tune.

There always should be sufficient practice time allotted early in pre-season drills so a package of signs is well understood. They should be used in intra-squad games, with coaches on the baselines performing their duties as if it were a regular season game. They should also be used in drills, if possible, by setting up a drill as part of batting practice—if time permits—where a batter and coach work together. The coach can say, "Okay, there is a runner on second, one out," and while the batting practice pitcher waits, the coach flashes the sign to the hitter. The pitcher then delivers the ball and the batter reacts under simulated game conditions.

Another technique, if time and facilities permit, is to verbally set up a game condition, then flash the signs and ask a player what he would do as a hitter or base runner. This forces the player to think in terms of what he might expect in a given tactical situation, and then forces him to recognize what he would be called upon to do. A coach should do this with every player, under all conceivable situations, until he is certain that his players know the signs and are comfortable with them.

   A note of caution: It is easier to change one sign, or how it is given, than to expect an entire team to change or be forced to cope with a difficult package. If a coach sees that his system is not getting across, then he should review it with an eye out for that first and only commandment of which we spoke earlier: simplicity.

GIVING THE SIGNS

   Depending upon the level of competition, some coaches wish to flash their own signs from the bench; others will flash them to a base line coach, who will relay them to the hitter and runner, as is done in the major leagues. It has become commonplace for coaches and managers to flash signs to their base line coaches: The first base coach gives signs to the right-

SIMPLIFIED OFFENSIVE PACKAGE: A = alert; I = indicator; H = hot sign;
D = decoy; V = validator or activator; RO = rub-off; R = release; TA = turn-away.
Referring back to Figure 1, you will note that the hot sign in this case is a ''take.''

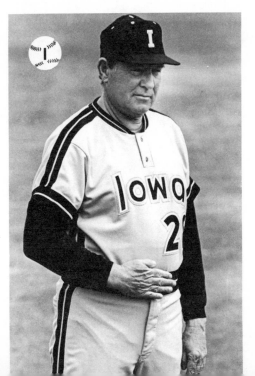

handed batters, who look directly at him from their spot in the batting box, and the third base coach gives signs to the left-handed hitters. Of course, some still prefer to have a third base coach flash the signs, which means a right-handed hitter must look around, either while in the box or by stepping out, to get his signs.

Regardless of the preference, the same people should give the signs all the time. This ensures a continuity in which the players are accustomed to the coach's rhythm and feel comfortable whenever they read his signals. It is amazing what happens when this responsibility is changed or split among different people. The rhythm of each will differ, and many times, a batter and runner will be unsure of whether the sign has been given and will ask for repeats; or, worse yet, they may miss it or mistake it altogether.

Coaches also should be good actors, fully content to produce a non-stop flurry of motions. Even if there is no play called, they should go through some routine on every pitch, being sure in the first couple of innings that they touch every area of the package. The reason for that is almost self-evident: If a coach touches the top half almost exclusively and then suddenly he goes to the bottom half, the guy on the other bench is going to say, "Wait a minute! Something's on here."

SIMPLIFIED OFFENSIVE PACKAGE: (continued)

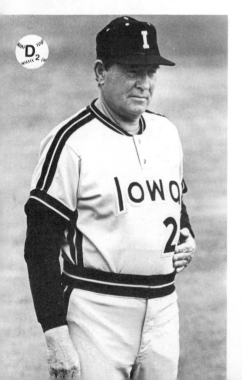

This can become a cat-and-mouse game. In going through all of those motions, they can give signs and rub them off, and they can do a lot of meaningless gestures. But all the while they are doing something and the guy on the other bench is trying to figure it out.

But no matter what they are doing, they must do it, as I noted earlier, with the same rhythm and must not vary their routine or the pace that is a part of these movements. Players also must respond—do a bit of acting themselves—to these actions as if they are getting a sign so that when it does come, there is no obvious change.

What about *changing signs*? This is one question I am continually asked. How often…and how do you do it to avoid confusion?

If a coach uses the block system, the signs tend to be consistent, and you can imagine what chaos could result if I moved the sacrifice from my left hip to the upper right chest, the bunt from the upper right chest to my midriff, and a take sign from the midriff to the upper left chest. The best way to change either the block or the holding packages is to move the indicator, or alter the interval between the indicator and the hot sign. It could be that a team will start the season with the second sign after the indicator as "hot." That can be changed to become the first sign after the indicator. Thus, the

various components of both packages stay in place and do not have to be relearned with all of the involved risks.

Signs can even be changed in mid-game—while a man is at bat, in fact. All that is required is a sign that switches the hot sign. Let's say that the indicator is one hand to the right side of the chest, and the hot sign for that is the first touch after that indicator. Now, when I put two hands to my chest, that means we have changed to the second sign after the indicator. That is all a part of the package, though it helps lessen the chance of a missed sign if the team is alerted that a change may be coming so they will be looking for it.

TAKING THE SIGNS

The proper time for a batter to take a sign from the coach is when he is approaching the plate and before he steps into the batter's box; also, just after each pitch is thrown to him while he is at bat. Remember, most pitchers use ten to fifteen seconds between pitches, so the action will begin immediately after he either has swung at the pitch or the ball plunks into the catcher's mitt. The batter must be alert so he can take the sign and be set for the pitch.

Now comes an important function of the batter—he must, as we noted earlier, continue to look through the sign after he receives it, either until he is given the release sign or the rub-off, or until the coach finishes his sequence and turns away or stops. Base runners, during this time, should be standing on their base while the sign is being given and they should start watching the sign-giver as they return to the bag. Both must be nonchalant in the way in which they take the sign so as not to tip it to the opponents. We will see later in the book how the opposition looks for the slightest hesitation, or other unnecessary action, to get a clue as to what the sign means.

REPEAT SIGN

Now, if the batter has missed the sign or cannot understand it, he should ask for it again by flashing a "repeat" sign, which is a part of the signs package. The best procedure is for the batter to step out of the box, look at the coach and make the repeat sign. The sign could be an equipment adjustment or a wipe of the hands, but he should pay attention as the sign is being repeated by looking directly at the coach. If the message still is unclear, he should call time out and talk to the coach to get the sign.

Batters also can be given a sign to use if they want the coach to repeat the signal. It can be something as simple as rubbing their hand down the middle of their shirt, but it should not be a part of their batting routine, such as a hitch of the pants, taking off the cap, drying their hands on the sides of their pants, or tapping a bat.

I firmly believe in the use of the release sign at all times to allay problems, because it lessens confusion and forces the batter to continue to look through all of the sequences and be certain that he knows what to do.

DEFENSE AND PITCHING

Thus far, I have talked about the various means by which offensive signs are given to batters and runners. But the defensive side of the game is equally important. There is a package of signs for the fielder and another between pitcher and catcher.

The fielder's signs can be signalled from the bench, or between players in certain situations, and some of the latter are verbal. Most signs flashed from the bench concern the actions that the defense will take to cope with runners on base, particularly when the coach senses the opposition may

TAKING THE SIGNS

REPEAT SIGN

be using a double steal tactic and he wishes to employ pickoffs or specific defenses to counter those moves. We will discuss in greater detail all of the most widely used defenses, and how they can be signalled, later in the book. For now it should suffice to say that coaches must be willing to give equal attention to this phase of their sign and signals system.

The signs between pitchers and catchers are as common as those between the coach and the batter and runner. But they also are a specific system of calls, which we will detail later in the book. These are not limited to pitcher and catcher and are totally integrated into the team defense. That, more than anything else, says it all about the overall importance of signs and signals: They are a total team function and a special language that must be understood by every player if the team—and I will stress again and again the team aspects of the game—is to be successful.

COACHES' QUIZ

1. Baseball signs are a form of:

   a. communication
   b. strategy
   c. plays
   d. all of the above

2. The most intricate system of signs and signals are between the head coach (or manager) on bench and:

   a. third base coach
   b. batter
   c. pitcher
   d. all of the above

3. The best signs and signals are done with:

   a. simplicity
   b. hand
   c. eye
   d. all of the above

4. The best system of signals for lower level coaches is:

   a. word signs and block
   b. holding system and flash system
   c. holding system and block system
   d. all of the above

5. The best time to give a signal is by:

   a. facing the batter directly
   b. walking toward the batter
   c. both

6. The obvious drawback to this package is that the signs can be:

   a. lost
   b. forgotten
   c. stolen
   d. all of the above

7. The sign package should be installed:

   a. last
   b. any time
   c. as quickly as possible
   d. all of the above

8. A very fundamental approach begins with just two signs:

   a. the indicator and bunt
   b. indicator and hot sign
   c. hot sign and bunt
   d. all of the above

9. The _____ relieves confusion and assists the hitter.

   a. first sign
   b. last sign
   c. release sign
   d. none of the above

CHAPTER 2

BUNT SIGNS: SACRIFICE AND SUICIDE SQUEEZE

For most teams, the bunting game is an integral part of their offensive philosophy. Certainly, the use of the sacrifice bunt is one of the most common ways to move runners along a base when a key run might be needed. But the bunt also can be a surprise tactic used to cross up a defense or begin a rally.

Of course, there are teams with great hitters who will disdain the use of the bunt, but those are few and far between. And there are teams that use this tactic as a primary weapon.

Several years ago I was coaching the United States team in an international series in Japan and learned firsthand that often the bunting game is more than an occasional tactic—that it can be *the* tactic.

In the bottom of the first inning, the Japanese team had its first four hitters bunting or using the fake-bunt, hit-away tactic to get base hits. They would look at the positioning of our infielders and if the first and third basemen were playing back, they would bunt. If our fielders came in, the Japanese batter would pivot and show the bunt, then pivot back and slash the ball through the drawn-in infield. We certainly weren't prepared for these tactics, and by the end of the first inning they were ahead 4-0. Finally, we decided the defense had to dictate so we made our third baseman charge as if he was looking for the bunt, then pull up sharply and hold his position. The Japanese players then could not figure out what we were doing, and the pressure was on them to do something they couldn't, or didn't wish to, do. We'll look at some of those tactics later in the book, but the point here is that the bunt, in some situations, can almost be considered an open-ended weapon, and I was curious as to how the Japanese saw its use against us.

"We can't match your team in power," the Japanese coach told me, "so we did the thing we do best, and that is to take advantage of our bunting ability, speed, and your defensive setup at that time. We do not have physically powerful players here, so we have to find other ways to create offense."

And creating offense is the best reason for using the bunt. Much depends on the level of baseball and the players' skills. In the major leagues, you rarely see teams use the bunting game in the early innings, though I recall hearing of Billy Martin, when he managed the Yankees, squeezing home a run in the first inning of a game at Yankee Stadium.

After the game, someone asked him about the play. Martin, never one to go by any "book," had a ready answer, and it made sense to me.

"I wanted to jump out on top and put the pressure on them to catch us," he said. "One run doesn't seem like much, but you're still ahead and that can sometimes cause people to get away from their game."

There are times when a coach knows it's going to be one of those days when every run will count, or when his best pitcher is going against the other team's best pitcher. If he has an opportunity to utilize the bunting game in any way, to get a run in the first or second inning, it could mean a victory.

Some teams will be like the Japanese, with speed on the base paths and batters who are adept at bunting. These features become an integral part of their offense because they most likely will not have many big innings, and therefore must make every opportunity work for them.

This decision is one only the coach can make, but he should determine his team's offensive capabilities as early as he can after beginning his practices. If he sees that he (a) will need the bunting game to help produce offense, and (b) has players who can execute it, it should be immediately installed.

Sure, you can have one without the other, but the coach had better hope that he has the players who can do it. Otherwise, he either must go through an intensive teaching phase to create these kinds of players—not an impossible task with players who are in the spirit of their team—or find another way to score runs.

Either way, once a coach determines that the bunting game must become a part of his strategy, he should begin working immediately to perfect it. This includes installing the signs as part of his package, and that can mean a different sign for each of the most common uses of the bunt: sacrifice, suicide squeeze, safety squeeze, run-and-bunt, bunt-and-run, and the drag bunt. That is like the menu from a Chinese restaurant in that the coach may not want to use every one because he may not have the talent to make all of them work. Then he must choose those that will work for him.

But make the determination as early as possible. Install the signs and then use both in all the drills and practices—even if a team might only occasionally use those plays—being sure that periodic work is done on them throughout the season. I can tell you from experience that if you let this slip, and decide only after the season has started that it should be a part of the signs package, there will be problems. Players simply are not tuned to these late additions and they often become the one area where mental errors occur.

If nothing else, bunting plays do give a team flexibility in its offense, and as we noted—and as the Japanese proved to us—it can be a surprise weapon that, when judiciously used, produces results.

Here are the five types of bunting situations and how they can be used and integrated in the signs package:

1. **Sacrifice:** The basic idea of a sacrifice bunt is for the batter to give himself up in order that a base runner may advance, either from first to second, from second to third, or both. The batter should bunt the ball only if it

SACRIFICE BUNT: A = alert; I = indicator; H = hot sign; D = decoy; V = validator; R = release; TA = turn-away.

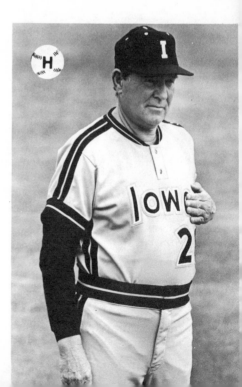

The Specifics

There are eight basic factors that a coach should consider as a part of his philosophy on using the bunt:

(1) Whether the team is home or away
(2) The score
(3) The inning
(4) The situation with outs and men on base
(5) Upcoming hitters and skills of each
(6) Baserunning skills of runners on base, and those of upcoming hitters for each particular situation
(7) Bench players available for pinch-hitting and pinch-running
(8) Opposition's fielding skills on special plays

is a low strike and must be certain that the ball is hit on the ground, but not so hard that it can be turned into a force out or, worse still, a double play.

The batter must check the defensive position of both the first and third basemen and know their capabilities for fielding bunts, along with that of the pitcher. Then he can put the ball on the ground where it has the best chance of succeeding.

Much depends on the situation. Ideally, the bunt should be laid down along the first base line because the first baseman is charged with holding the runner and will get to it late enough for the runner to reach second base. Yet the bunter must be certain that he puts the ball far enough away from the pitcher where he cannot field it, turn, and throw out the runner at second base. He also must be wary of the third baseman who will be charging in with the pitch and also, if he gets to the ball quickly enough, can get a force out—or start a double play.

If there is a runner on second base and the first baseman has no runner to worry about, he will come hurtling toward the plate with the pitch and will be in a good position to throw out the runner at third. The best I ever saw at this was a first baseman named Ferris Fain, who played for the old

SACRIFICE BUNT: (continued)

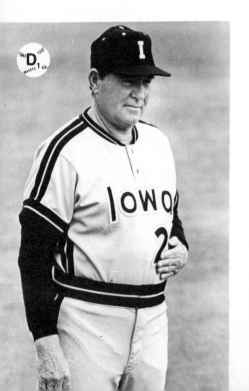

Philadelphia A's and Chicago White Sox in the '50s. He was a left-handed thrower and was absolutely deadly in getting bunts and throwing out runners at third. He earned the nickname "Fearless Ferris" with his exploits, but he forced opponents to dump their bunts, in these situations, along the third base line.

We will discuss later in this chapter how these aggressive fielding tendencies can be countered.

The time for this maneuver is dictated by the coach's view of the game, with regards to his team's talent and that of the opposition. We have noted how it can be used to get an early lead when there appears to be a tight pitcher's duel, or if a team is not offensively strong. Mostly, it is used late in a game when a team is tied or a run behind, but the coach must know whether his players can execute the maneuver.

Since the coach has the sign for the sacrifice in his package, he can use it on the first pitch to the hitter; or he can use it on a 2-and-0 count when the pitcher will be trying to throw a strike. Often a coach will signal for a sacrifice bunt after allowing a hitter to swing at the first pitch, if only because of the psychological lift that it gives to the hitter. Hitters want to hit and be given a chance to do so. Asking a hitter to deliberately make an out without the chance of at least getting a hit often is a negative. But when it's late in the

Bobby Bragan, a former major league player and manager, and minor and major league executive, never has been shy about expressing his opinions on baseball's stratagems. Nor has he ever been shy about throwing away the book and taking a fresh look at every situation.

Several years ago he expounded on the use of the sacrifice bunt:

"The most stereotyped play in the game is the sacrifice bunt in two common situations. Most managers feel they cannot go wrong calling it with a runner on first base with none out; or there are men on first and second with less than two out and the pitcher is due to hit. In my book, a manager hardly can do worse than give away an out to advance the runners one base."

The main reason, Bragan reasoned, was the livelier baseball being used, and which he believed had a definite effect on the bunt and how far it traveled before being fielded. "It is my distinct impression," he added, "that the runner on first is cut down at second on one out of three attempted sacrifices."

No one—not even a Hall of Fame player—is immune to messing up a bunt signal.

SUICIDE SQUEEZE:
Batter's acknowledgment sign

game and a win is at stake, a player must be willing to perform his duty at the plate—to make a sacrifice.

2. **Suicide Squeeze:** This play is just what its name signifies: Either the runner at third and the batter succeed or the runner is a dead duck (figuratively, of course).

Both the batter and the runner have "grave" responsibilities. The runner must not tip off the play. He cannot start for the plate too soon, or he'll either be picked off or be an easy out because the pitcher will knock down the hitter with a high inside pitch and the catcher can easily apply the tag.

The runner should wait until the pitcher's front foot hits the ground, or until his pitching arm starts to come through with the throw. If the runner has a walking lead and has his weight forward, he can get going quickly.

Now the burden is on the batter, who must make contact with the ball, regardless of where it is pitched. Bunting technique doesn't matter here, but he must be certain that he doesn't tip off the play by turning his body, or bat, before the ball is pitched. And he must be sure the ball goes into the ground when it is bunted, but not too hard toward the pitcher, who has the easiest throw to the catcher.

Many feel this kind of play is a no-no early in the game, but I like the surprise element, especially if it is done with no outs, or if the pitcher pays little attention to the runner at third base. In the late innings, the opposition may be looking for it, so the third baseman is liable to hold the man closer at third, and the pitcher may go from a holdback position so he can deliver the ball quickly.

If a coach feels he will use this play—even just two or three times during the season—he should put it in at the start of practice and have his sign as part of the package, along with an *acknowledgment sign* from the batter to the runner after the coach has given the signal. That acknowledgment sign can be nothing more than taking his bottom hand off the bat or lifting a cap—something to let the runner know that the play will be executed. The coach should give a *verbal sign* to the runner (such as his first name or number) at the same time and the runner should acknowledge the sign, either verbally or with a simple visual sign such as tugging at his belt buckle or rubbing the side of his pants. Those signs, too, are installed at the very start, and reviewed from time to time.

3. **Safety Squeeze:** This counts on the element of surprise and has, in my mind, one big drawback: It is a defensive play because the runner at third base does not go home unless the ball is bunted, and the batter only bunts if the pitch is a strike. A coach also is lassoed a bit because he must be certain that he has a speedy runner at third base who can beat a throw home,

SUICIDE SQUEEZE: Runner's acknowledgment sign

and an adept bunter who can put the ball where a play at home will be difficult.

Some coaches will use the sacrifice sign for this play, since all the elements are the same, though a coach may wish to make it a permanent part of his package and use it on such occasions as the first pitch to a batter after a runner reaches third, or on a 2-and-0 count when the pitcher will try to throw a strike. No acknowledgment of the sign is needed.

Regardless of which squeeze play is used, the coach should weigh two factors: 1) Is this run important enough to use such a bang-bang play; and 2) how closely is the pitcher checking the runner at third base (to allow him the leeway to get a jump toward home)?

4. *Run-and-Bunt:* I like this maneuver because it can succeed in two ways: The runner and the hitter both can be on base after the play; or, even if the batter misses the ball, the runner can steal a base. This is aggressive baseball, and while it is desirable to have a fast runner on base, a quick start by the base runner and a well-placed bunt can allow even a slow runner to advance.

Still, there are two prevailing theses about the use of the run-and-bunt. One is that the bunter should protect the runner as he does in the suicide squeeze, and make contact with the pitch any way he can; the other is that the bunter need *not* make contact with the pitch unless it is a strike, and let the runner take his chances of getting a stolen base. That is a coach's preference, which he must determine from the abilities of his players. But regardless of which rationale he uses, he should instruct his runner not to tip off the play, or to go until the pitcher has started his arm toward the plate. Again, a good body lean combined with a walking start will get him going a bit quicker.

This play is exciting in that it can create an extra base for the speedy runner if the third baseman is forced to field the bunt. If the third baseman can't get back, or if the shortstop or catcher are slow in covering the bag, then the play becomes a two-base bonus. But the bunter must make the third baseman field the ball.

A good time to call the play is when the pitcher is behind in the count, with none out and a runner on first base. It can be part of the signs package but it does not need an acknowledgment since the stolen base is a possibility and the missed strike will not be an automatic out.

5. *Drag Bunt:* Another fine player from the '50s and early '60s, Nelson Fox of the A's, White Sox, and Orioles, was a master of this play, which is used to get a base hit. He succeeded twenty-eight out of thirty-four tries one season, which adds a lot of sure hits to a player's totals. He had the

RUN-AND-BUNT: Hot sign

Dumb Play

Roberto Clemente, the late Pirates star who finished his major league career with a .300 average, once went to bat in the ninth inning, with two out and none on, and his team trailing by a run. He proceeded to make the third out easily by getting tossed out on a poorly executed bunt.

"Bunting with nobody on base when we needed a run to tie was the dumbest play I've ever seen," his manager fumed at him after the game. "You must be loco to pull a boner like that. There was only one thing for you to do. You had to be up there swinging for a home run."

Clemente looked at him squarely in the eye and shrugged.

"Boss," he said, "me no feel like home run."

So much for signals.

ideal components: he was a fast, left-handed batter with exceptional bat control.

At the major league levels, players of this caliber often are on their own. But at lower levels, the coach should control the play with a definite sign. It can be an effective surprise weapon, and even if infielders are playing in and looking for a bunt, a good drag bunter can loft the ball over their heads.

A player's skill should determine whether it becomes a part of the signs package and coaches can suggest to their players that they get an indication before the man goes to bat that he can execute the play.

We've discussed the bunts amidst a flurry of charging infielders, and the latter often chill a coach's desire to run a good bunting game. However, there is a technique that will put the chill back on the infielders and open up room for a more effective bunting game:

6. ***Fake Bunt-and-Hit:*** The play works off a bit of deception by the batter—he will pivot and show the bunting position, but, in an instant, slide the top hand from the middle of the bat barrel back to join the bottom hand in a hitting position.

At the same time, the batter brings the bat to his shoulder to get bat control because all he wants to do is make contact and get the ball past the charging infielders—anywhere past them, it doesn't matter.

A short, compact swing will do it. If the ball is to go to the right side, the batter, if he is right-handed, turns clockwise and brings his hands forward so that when he swings, he drags the barrel through his motion. If he wants to go to the other side, he keeps his stance open as soon as the bat goes to the hitting position, and stays at a 45-degree angle and in the direction in which the ball will be hit.

When is this play used?

Let's take a hypothetical situation. With a runner on first, a sacrifice bunt isn't appropriate because of an aggressive defense. Instead of the sacrifice we want the movement of that hard-charging defense to create some holes. If it works, we have two runners on base instead of one. The infielders, suddenly seeing a ball come whistling at them, also might be a bit more cautious the next time, and this gives the bunting game more room to operate.

COACHES' QUIZ

1. One of the most common ways to advance runners is by the:

    a. bunt
    b. hit-and-run
    c. squeeze play
    d. none of the above

2. Bunting plays give a team:

    a. easy outs
    b. flexibility
    c. rigid offense
    d. none of the above

3. A sacrifice bunt should be laid down the:

    a. third base line
    b. back toward the pitcher
    c. first base line
    d. none of the above

4. The suicide squeeze is used to:

    a. get a hit
    b. make an out
    c. score a run
    d. none of the above

5. The run-and-bunt is:

    a. defensive strategy
    b. safe strategy
    c. aggressive strategy
    d. none of the above

6. Bunt-and-run is considered:

    a. defensive strategy
    b. safe strategy
    c. aggressive strategy
    d. none of the above

7. The drag bunt is used to:

    a. get a base hit
    b. advance the runner
    c. squeeze the runner
    d. none of the above

8. In using the fake bunt-and-hit, the hitter should use a:

    a. full swing
    b. short, compact swing
    c. bunt technique
    d. none of the above

CHAPTER 3
HIT-AND-RUN/RUN-AND-HIT

The hit-and-run play, as an offensive weapon, is well known, throughout baseball, but the reverse action—the run-and-hit—may be less recognized as a top offensive tool. Often it is misidentified and everything that happens with a batter and hitter working in tandem is grouped under the hit-and-run label.

That is too bad, in my estimation, because I favor the run-and-hit play as a better tactic, particularly at lower levels of competition, because it does not require the particular skill of having a right-handed batter with great bat control who can put the ball on the ground behind a runner going from first base. With the run-and-hit play, the batter is called on simply to hit the ball—anyplace.

Let's look at more specific differences between the two plays.

HIT-AND-RUN

The hit-and-run does exactly what it says: The batter must hit the ball after the runner takes off. But the key is getting it on the ground and behind the runner. The second baseman will move to cover the bag, and as he moves, the ball will be hit into the territory he just has vacated. The runner, if he has good speed, then has a chance to reach third base; and even if the batter misses the pitch, he could steal second, though he would have to be a very speedy runner because in order not to tip off the play. However, he is "thinking steal" and must be prepared to slide into second base if the batter swings and misses.

Hotshot Idea

There are seven basic factors that a coach should consider as a part of his philosophy on the use of hit-and-run and run-and-hit plays:

(1) Whether the team is home or away
(2) The score
(3) The inning
(4) The situation with outs and men on base
(5) Upcoming hitters and skills of each
(6) Baserunning skills of runners then on base, and of upcoming hitters for each particular situation
(7) Your pitcher's fatigue factor

Bobby Bragan, the former major and minor league manager and executive, never was at a loss for

The purpose of this play is to advance the runner at least one base. And if the play really works—with a fast runner, or with a ball so well placed that it must be chased down by the rightfielder—he can get to third base. It also can protect a runner on first base from the double play if the ball is not properly placed because the runner will have a little more of a jump than if he had gone only after the ball had been hit. However, the play generally is employed with a slower runner on base, and the batter should think at all times of protecting the runner by making contact with the ball, and not of the runner getting a stolen base.

Some major league managers, such as the late Walter Alston and Paul Richards, were great devotees of this play. Alston called it "one of the greatest plays in baseball," even Al Lopez, an exponent of power baseball made such extensive use of it in 1959 that he took the Chicago White Sox to the American League pennant by utilizing speed, a group of bat control hitters, and a tough pitching corps that could win with a one- or two-run edge that this play so often got him.

So much of the play's success depends on the hitter, and truly good hit-and-run men are real artists with the bat. Bobby Hofman, who went from

HIT-AND-RUN: A = alert; I = indicator; H = hot sign; D = decoy; V = validator; R = release; TA = turn-away.

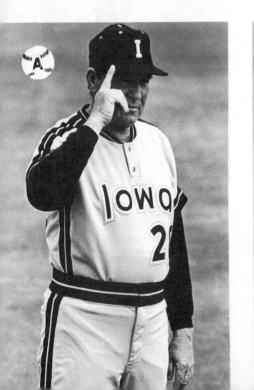

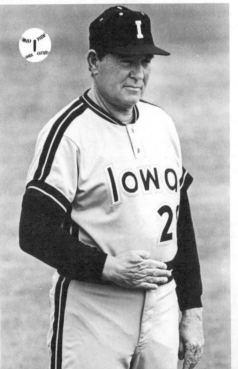

the playing field to the executive ranks in major league baseball, says that his former manager, Bill Rigney, taught him a technique that helped make Hofman one of the great hit-and-run men, and extended his playing career because of it. Of course, Rigney was in the same mold, and when he managed, his teams were famous for their use of the play.

"Bill taught me to just keep my right elbow into my side so I cannot get the bat out in front of my body," Hofman says. "That means you lead with your hands. The hands are out in front and you just try to hit the ball to right field." You can get the same effect—dragging the bat barrel—by pushing the front arm so the back elbow moves along from the back hip to the front of the stomach. One commandment for the batter: He must hit the ball, even if it means throwing his bat at a pitch that is far out of the strike zone, in order to protect the runner.

When is a good time to use the play?

I've always liked it in the middle or late stages of a game, but there is no hard-and-fast rule if a team has the right player mix to get it accomplished. I think two ideal situations would be on 2-and-0 or 3-and-1 pitches because the batter, if he swings and misses, still will be at bat and will have a chance of

an opinion—even if it touched some of baseball's most time-honored plays. Here is his opinion of the hit-and-run play:

"One of the most overworked plays in baseball is the hit-and-run, which is part of the basic strategy of every manager and coach. Now the hit-and-run is a fine play but it has two serious drawbacks. It sharply reduces the batter's chances of a base hit, and it succeeds in pushing up the runner on a ground ball only 30 percent of the time, and then at the cost of a big out.

"The hit-and-run is a typical example of an old-fashioned stratagem that has long outlived its usefulness. I don't doubt it was a hotshot idea when John J. McGraw,

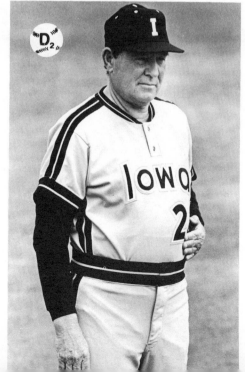

Willie Keeler, and Hughey Jennings dreamed it up so many years ago. In that low-scoring era, when games generally were decided by one run, giving away an out to advance a runner a base might have been a good trade. Today it's a lousy swap, especially in an early inning, because it cuts heavily into a team's potential for getting a big cluster of runs.

''In the majority of cases, the batter is saddled with pretty severe handicaps. He's obliged to swing at the ball, whether the pitch is good or bad, to protect the runner going down to second. Too often that results in easy outs. And if he is a right-handed hitter, he cramps his natural power by pushing the ball to right field, the opposite direction of his free swing.''

getting a good pitch. I like to give the batter the option in these instances and, even with the play on and the runner moving, of taking ball four. There now are two runners on base, which is what we wanted in the first place.

There are several dangers a coach should consider before calling this play:

1. Both players or just one, could miss the sign, and the runner might be caught.

2. The batter could be forced to swing at a bad pitch to protect the runner.

3. The hitter could lace a line drive into a quick double play.

4. An inexperienced runner could be in trouble if he falls for some decoy tricks by an infielder, such as the latter pretending to get into position for a ground ball when, in fact, the ball has been hit in the air. Runners must be taught to look at the batter's action after their third step toward the base.

5. The hitter simply does not make contact with the pitch and the runner is hung up.

Some coaches advocate using the play with a 3-and-1 count, but if a batter must swing regardless of the pitch, he well may be lunging after ball

HIT-AND-RUN: (continued)

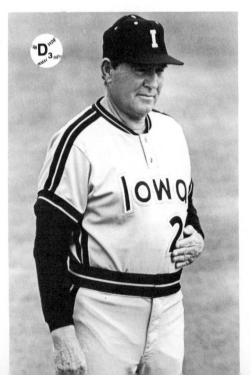

four. Thus, instead of a certain two runners on base, any of the negatives listed above could occur.

However, the play certainly merits consideration after a pitcher has just walked a batter, or if he is at a 2-and-0 count on a hitter and tries to get the next pitch into the strike zone.

THE SIGNS

There is a degree of flexibility in the signs required for making the hit-and-run play successful. I like to use the play in tandem with a good base runner and a crafty hitter because the chances are it will not break down or end in disaster. That means the two can have a sign between them, or they can get it from the coach.

In the former case, the hitter will flash to the runner that he wants to try a hit-and-run. Here, the *acknowledge sign* must be a part of the package, and it can be anything, as we discussed previously, that the parties will see and understand. Normally, this kind of independence comes only at the high levels of competition where the coach or manager has ultimate faith in the competence of the two players.

When the coach institutes the sign, it will also carry an acknowledgment sign between batter and runner. This, of course, will be part of the team's package and will be integrated from the early days of practice so that everyone will be familiar with both signs. As with all other parts of this package, it should be practiced and periodically reviewed, though a team using the hit-and-run with any frequency will also have to be certain that the signs are not being stolen.

RUN-AND-HIT

The run-and-hit play is more to my liking because it has greater flexibility, particularly at lower levels of competition where batters do not have great bat control. Simply put, with the run-and-hit, the runner takes off immediately, just as if he were stealing, because the hitter has only one mission: Hit the ball...anyplace. There is no attempt to deceive the second baseman by moving him out of position, though if the batter is truly clever, he can execute what amounts to the hit-and-run; with the runner already on the move, chances are a ball hit into right field will easily land the runner at third

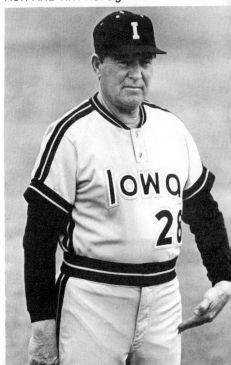

RUN-AND-HIT: Hot sign

base. Better still, a well-placed hit, combined with good speed, could get him all the way home.

Even if the batter doesn't hit the ball, the runner could get a stolen base on the play because he will have such a quick jump. The batter also can be more discriminating on his selection of pitches, the idea of the play being that the runner will be running and the hitter will be hitting *only* if he gets a good pitch. That is a matter of personal choice by a coach. Some may want the play called and executed, regardless of where the pitch is located.

I like the play when the batter has counts of 2-and-0, 2-and-2, and—if given a green light—3-and-1 and 3-and-2, because in each instance, the pitcher probably will be looking to throw a strike, and the batter will have a better selection and drive it for a hit. The worst thing that can happen on this play is for the batter to break down and take a pitch right down the middle. The play also has the advantage, on balls hit to the infield, of preventing a double play, because the runner will have gotten such an early break.

THE SIGNS

Like the hit-and-run, the sign can be flashed between hitter and runner only, or it can come from the bench. Again, the *acknowledge* signal should be part of this package for a greater chance of success. I believe the coach should control this kind of play at the lower levels and he can make it a part of his package from his early practice sessions.

However, he must be certain to discriminate it from his regular steal sign and his players should be well schooled in the various differences and situations when the steal and the run-and-hit will be used. This also should be reviewed periodically throughout the season.

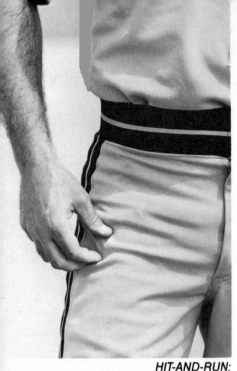

HIT-AND-RUN:
Runner's acknowledgment

HIT-AND-RUN: Batter's acknowledgment

COACHES' QUIZ

1. The better of the two offensive weapons is:

   a. the hit-and-run
   b. the run-and-hit

2. In the hit-and-run the batter:

   a. must hit the baseball
   b. has the option of hitting the ball
   c. must take
   d. none of the above

3. The principle of the hit-and-run is to:

   a. fool the catcher
   b. fool the pitcher
   c. open a hole in the defense
   d. none of the above

4. The purpose of this play is to:

   a. steal a base
   b. fool the defense
   c. advance the runner
   d. all of the above

5. So much of the success of the hit-and-run depends on:

   a. the pitcher
   b. the runner
   c. the hitter
   d. all of the above

6. The best time to use the hit-and-run is:

   a. early in the game
   b. in the middle of the game
   c. when one or more runs behind
   d. none of the above

7. On the run-and-hit the batter will only hit if he:

   a. is ahead of the count
   b. gets a good pitch
   c. is behind in the count
   d. none of the above

CHAPTER 4
TAKE OR HIT AWAY

Should the batter "take" the pitch...or should the batter hit it?

Those are two of the most perplexing problems that a coach faces in every game, and the answer every time is dictated by a number of factors that all must be considered within a few seconds.

It often isn't as easy as it seems, mainly because a coach's personal philosophy comes into play. Some coaches believe they should control almost every pitch to a batter, and therefore continually go through the take/hit sequence of signs. I'm not one of those. My cardinal rule is: Don't take the bat out of the batter's hands.

I believe this for a couple of reasons. First, the hitter is at the plate to do what he probably can do best—hit the ball. This requires almost as much psychological skill—the power of positive thinking—as it does reflex action, and if the batter constantly has to check to see if he is allowed to hit, he won't have a very good attitude about his ability.

This leads to the second reason: Players who don't feel good about their skills soon become discouraged and this impacts on their play. I'm certain that every coach has been through this, and soon realizes that players who are in the spirit of the occasion also are in the spirit of their team. How a coach controls his players' skills will have a lot to say about this.

I'm not advocating that there is not a time and place to use hit and take signs, because in every game they become part of the strategic considerations. My preference is to limit their use to specific times when it may be to my batter's—and my team's—advantage.

I believe there are six instances when the take considerations must be made.

1. A very wild pitcher makes the take sign become almost automatic on 2-and-0, 3-and-0 and 3-and-1 counts, or after he has just walked a batter on four or five pitches.

Obey or Be Damned

There are nine obvious factors that a coach should consider as a part of his basic philosophy on taking or hitting away:

(1) Whether the team is home or away
(2) The score
(3) The inning
(4) The situation with outs and men on base
(5) Your pitcher's fatigue factor
(6) Your bullpen strength
(7) Opposing pitcher's fatigue and control
(8) Opposition's bullpen strength
(9) Opposition's fielding skills on special plays.

Obedience to a coach's signs can be a double-edged sword.

Take the case of movie star Chuck Connors, who once was an aspiring first baseman with the Chicago Cubs, then managed by Phil Cavaretta.

The Cubs were playing the New York Giants in New York's Polo Grounds, and Connors was sent up to pinch-hit against Sal Maglie. The count went to 3-and-1, and there were two men on base, with Chicago behind by two runs.

Connors had a brainstorm. Everyone in the ball park, including Maglie, would figure that Cavaretta would flash the take sign on the next pitch, and that Sal would throw a "safe" fastball down the middle to get the strike.

Sure enough, Connors got the take sign. He recalls:

2. A four-ball walk by a pitcher not normally too wild often can mean that he has "lost it" and that can happen to any pitcher, at any time in a game.

3. The first two batters have each gone out on first ball pitches. Suddenly life has become too easy for the pitcher. Make him work again.

4. Your team is behind and it is getting late in the game. Consider that the pitcher may be getting tired and you want to work him a bit harder to get a base runner or good pitches to hit. Here it is important to know the limitations of the opposition's pitching corps. At lower levels of competition, a team may have only one good pitcher, so you want to get rid of him and bring on lesser talent. Or a team may have a good relief pitcher, so you want to take as much advantage of the starter as you can till he is gone.

5. You need base runners. This means the hitters aren't hitting on their own, so the coach must take control and make them be more selective, or get the pitcher in a hole where he must deliver better pitches or walk more batters.

6. When a team is behind and needs to start some offense.

TAKE: A = alert; I = indicator; H = hot sign; D = decoy; V = validator; R = release; TA = turn-away.

"I said to myself, 'Where are you really going? You're barely hanging on with this club, and here you've got a chance to be a hero. Are you going to let this chance pass you by?' Well, the answer was no, so Maglie pitched, I swung, and hit one into the right-field seats. It felt great and I really took my time trotting around the bases, because I knew what was waiting for me.

"When I got back to the dugout, there was Cavaretta really glaring at me. I just looked at him and said, 'Don't holler. I know you're mad, and I'm probably on my way back to the minor leagues.'

"I was correct, because the next day, I was gone...sent down for hitting a home run when I should have taken a pitch."

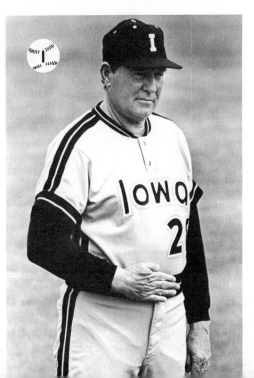
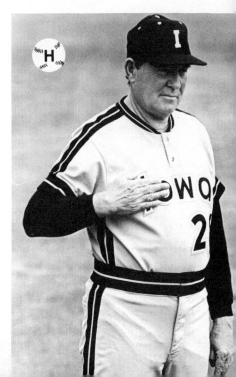

WHEN ARE YOU HITTING?

I believe batters are hitting every time they are at the plate—unless they have the take sign. That makes it easy for them, but still they must know they have some good options. Here are some considerations:

1. After a four-ball walk, we said above that the take sign can be in order. And it can—except, if the pitcher is not wild by nature, why not allow the hitter to go after the first pitch? You can bet the next pitch will be a strike, so give the batter the option of hitting it.

2. When the count is 2-and-0, 3-and-0, or 3-and-1, the take sign is apt to be flashed. But what is wrong with allowing the batter the option of going for a pitch he feels will be a strike? If it isn't, he can take it and get a walk, or put the pitcher deeper into the hole. However, if a coach gives a distinct hit signal to a batter on 3-and-0, the guy is apt to get itchy and swing at the pitch, regardless of what it is or where it is. Too often, 3-and-0 pitches become pop-ups, fair or foul, and an advantage is lost. If the batter is allowed to be under his own control, his judgment normally will be sound as to the pitch selection.

TAKE: (continued)

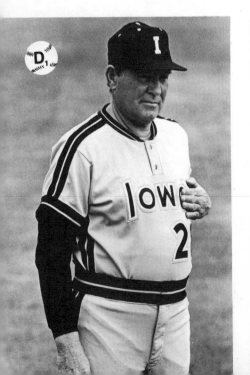

The best rule is to know the hitter and how he can react to something like a 3-and-0 pitch. Remember, if a power hitter is at the plate, looking at 3-and-0, the pitcher is no dummy, and he's not going to give him a fat pitch.

THE SIGNS

Hit: As we've noted, a batter is hitting, even when a team has definite hit signs, unless told otherwise. In other words, the rule is: Any time you don't get a take sign, you are hitting. However, in lower levels of competition, to underscore this action—and to reassure hitters who got 2-and-0, 3-and-0, or 3-and-1 counts and think they may have missed a take or hit sign—the hit sign can be flashed. Now he knows for certain what he can do and he won't worry about something else. The hitter's mind should be clear of everything but hitting.

If the batter has taken a called strike but still is ahead of the pitcher, you can give the hit sign for the next pitch. Much depends on the level of competition and the ability of the player. At higher levels, flashing the run-and-hit sign on 2-and-0 or 3-and-1 can be a consideration because the opposition, thinking the batter may be taking the pitch, may be caught by surprise.

HIT AWAY SIGN

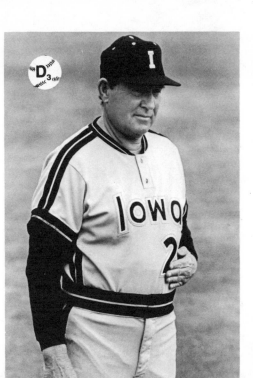

Strictly speaking, it is not a hit sign, but it utilizes the situation where the hit/take sequence is in the mind of the defense.

Take: Once the batter gets the take sign, he must not swing at the pitch, but again coaches should be judicious in its use so as not to make a robot of the batter. In many cases, a take sign is on until the coach either rubs it off or flashes a different sign. That is a matter of preference and is something that must be part of a team's signs package from its early practice sessions. A good note for lower levels: Batters should maintain their normal batting stance.

Both the hit and take signs can be worked in as part of the total sign package but they should be simple. At higher levels, coaches may institute a sequence of signs for take, hit, and steal, starting at the bill of the cap for "take," to the letters for "hit," and to the side for "steal." But whatever is clearest and easiest to understand is still the rule.

COACHES' QUIZ

1. One of the cardinal rules for a coach is:

    a. gave a hit/take sign on every pitch
    b. only give the hit/take sign when the batter is behind in the count
    c. don't take the bat out of the batter's hands
    d. none of the above

2. The take should be used when:

    a. the pitcher is wild
    b. the first two batters have each gone out on first two pitched baseballs
    c. both of the above

3. The major concern when allowing a batter to hit is to know that your batter:

    a. may swing if runner is trying to steal a base
    b. may not swing at all
    c. both of the above

4. Once the batter gets the take sign, he:

    a. has an option to swing only if the pitch is good
    b. may swing if runner is trying to steal a base
    c. may not swing at all
    d. all of the above

CHAPTER 5
STEALING SECOND AND THIRD

The use of the stolen base as part of a team's attack is a time-honored means of revving up an offense and weakening a defense. Done successfully, it can be an easier means of scoring runs, a compensation for lack of power hitting, and a truly exciting brand of play that is infectious throughout a team's roster. Its success also can harry a defense into errors, it can open holes for base hits when infielders "cheat" to cover the bases, and it can absolutely rattle a pitcher to the point where he gets behind hitters and makes pitching mistakes that can be turned into hits.

This tactic is especially effective at lower levels of competition where young pitchers may not have a good move to hold runners on base, where their delivery is a bit slow, and where catchers have not yet developed a strong and accurate throwing arm.

Of course, inserting this into an offense is strictly a call by the coach. Some may feel they do not have the personnel to make it work, but here I caution against being blinded by an overriding judgment based solely on speed considerations. The effective use of the stolen base often compensates for a lack of roadrunners—but it depends on what kind of steals are used, when used, and in what situations. My best advice is to have it as a part of your arsenal, and then use it to your advantage.

WHAT ARE THE CONSIDERATIONS?

There are a half dozen factors which must be considered when employing the steal:

1. **Speed of the Base Runner:** While very desirable, it is, as I just noted, not absolutely necessary to make the tactic work. However, if a team does have it, schooling players in the techniques and tactics is a must.

Swipe at Stunts

Bobby Bragan, who many have considered an avant-garde thinker in terms of baseball's traditional plays, called the steal of third base "the most neglected play in baseball."

"People carry on as though a guy has pulled a job as daring as the Brinks holdup when he swipes third," Bragan said. "Nuts. It's infinitely harder to steal second base, a stunt that doesn't get a ripple from the customers."

Bragan acknowledged that the throw to second base was 127 feet compared to just 90 feet to third base, but he also pointed out that extra distance is covered in less than half a second once the catcher throws the ball.

He further bulwarks his case by noting that a lead from first base generally is about five feet because the pitcher can snap a throw to first and get a pickoff. But runners at second take as much as fifteen feet, with little danger of a pickoff because the pitcher must make a wheeling motion to make his throw.

Okay, Bragan is told, but that can be lessened by having the shortstop move closer to second base and keep the runner closer to the bag.

The consequence of that, he countered, is a wider hole in the infield, with the resulting weakening of the defense. Then there is the

2. *The Score:* The common rule is to employ the steal when a team is ahead, tied, or not more than one run behind. But I prefer to look at each situation, number of outs, hitters coming up, runners' skills, and defense's skills, even when a team trails 5-0 in the early innings, if I think I can get away with it. Or if a team is behind by two runs but has a good runner on base, let him go. It can get things going, perhaps make a defense overly conscious of guarding the bases and rattle the pitcher into bad pitches. Often when a team gets ahead by a big, early lead, there is a lull and if a coach feels this could become a big sleep, then the stolen base wakes people up and gets the offense going again.

3. *Number of Outs:* Again, the "book" says no outs, or one out, but don't overlook special circumstances. If there is a fast runner on first base with two outs, but a good hitter at the plate, why not put the runner in position to score? A coach must look closely at the strengths and weaknesses of his lineup when making such commitments. If he has a man on and two good hitters coming up, chances are the opposing coach will choose to pitch to at least one of them. If he gets a stolen base, the first good hitter might come through; if he is walked, then the opposition, while hoping for a double play or force out, still has put itself in jeopardy of creating a big inning for the offense.

Of course, there are also possibilities for replacing poor hitters with good pinch-hitters when steals bring on run-scoring situations, or of canceling an opposition's move when it walks a batter to set up an out situation. It always has seemed to me that using the stolen base successfully often creates more problems than the opposition can solve.

4. *The Count:* There are good times, not-so-good times, and terrible times to try to steal. The good ones are on the first pitch to a batter, or with the count 1-and-0, 2-and-0, and 2-and-2; the not-so-good ones are at 3-and-1 and 3-and-2 where the batter must not swing at a bad ball; and the bad ones are 0-and-1, 0-and-2, and 3-and-0. At lower levels, the batter should protect the runner by placing his bat barrel over the plate but above the ball and then draw it back as the ball crosses the plate, perhaps delaying the catcher's throw. On any count on which the runner gets the steal sign, he should go only if he gets a good jump on the pitcher.

5. *The Pitcher:* You should consider his ability to hold a runner close to the bag, i.e., the effectiveness of his pickoff move. Coaches should try to figure out, from studying his pitching motion, when he will come to the plate with the ball, and when he will go to the base. If that can be called consistently, then the stealing pattern will take care of itself. But if a coach tells his players to wait until the pitch is made, his team won't get many stolen bases because any steal depends on the base runner getting a good jump.

6. **The Catcher:** Even if the pitcher has a good move to a base, if the catcher does not have a good release after he gets the ball, or a weak or inaccurate throwing arm, the steal is possible. At lower levels of competition, catchers are vulnerable.

STEALING A BASE

STRAIGHT STEAL: There are three possibilities—stealing second, third, and home.

1. **Stealing Second:** Can be done any time. With a right-handed pitcher on the mound, the runner should look for the "open shoulder," which occurs when he turns from the stretch position to throw to the plate. As soon as the runner sees that left shoulder move forward, he should take off.

Watch to see when the pitcher flexes his back foot because that nearly always indicates he is about to throw the pitch; or check his body lean toward the plate. They are tip-offs against right-handers.

STRAIGHT STEAL: A = alert; I = indicator; H = hot sign; D = decoy; V = validator; R = release; TA = turn-away.

case of the third baseman: He must play even with the bag to get the catcher's throw, and that, he said, makes him a "pushover" for a bunt.

"A team with a reputation for bold baserunning collects dividends that are not apparent in the box score by keeping the opposing pitcher and infield off balance," Bragan concluded.

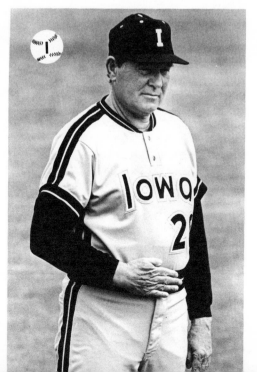
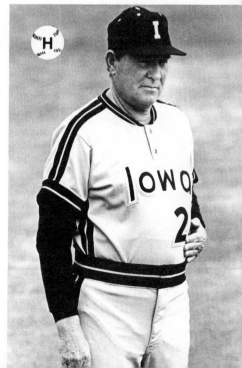

When a left-hander is on the mound, the best clue is the movement of his head, and whether it is toward the base or toward home plate. If the latter, he can be pretty certain the man is about to pitch.

2. ***Stealing Third:*** Rookie pitchers are vulnerable here. If a rookie gives just one glance at second, it is a dead giveaway that he won't make a play on the runner. If the infielder isn't holding him close, and if he has good running speed, then he can take off. The runner should also check the position of the third baseman and shortstop. If they play back, they are almost conceding him a stolen base, so take off. Then he is in position to score in any number of ways. Still, be mindful of the axiom: Don't make either the first or third out of any inning at third base.

3. ***Stealing Home:*** This really requires a player with great foot speed, though if there is a methodical pitcher who is lazy about checking the runner, a player with average speed could succeed. The coach must again make this judgment after studying the pitcher. A runner can set up the play with some false starts toward home, and thus lull the pitcher into thinking nothing will happen. On the third or fourth try, the runner goes after seeing the pitcher relax.

STRAIGHT STEAL: (continued)

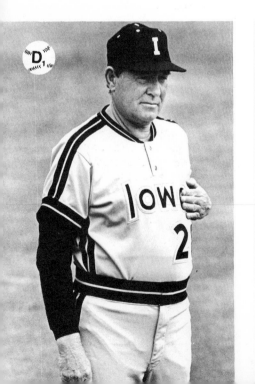

There are two important points in calling this play:

First, there must be an *acknowledgment sign* between runner and batter.

Second, the batter cannot swing at the pitch. His only move, if at all, could be a nonchalant step backward in the box, getting him closer to the catcher, and forcing the latter to move around him to make the tag on a runner who should be hook-sliding toward the front of the plate. However, the batter's move cannot be too obvious lest he tip off the catcher.

There also are a couple of techniques that are applicable in all of the above situations:

1. **The Batter:** Some coaches will have the batter protect the runner when he is stealing second or third—but not home—by not hitting the pitch, only looking to delay, for a moment, the catcher's throw. Others will have him fake a bunt, as we noted before, without making contact. Again, this does not apply to a steal of home. But I really don't favor either one because I don't want to put the batter in a hole by deliberately swinging for a strike; and I really wonder just how much a catcher is harassed into delaying his throw.

The Billyball

When Billy Martin became manager of the Oakland A's in 1980, he developed a style of baseball called "Billyball," because its aggressiveness mirrored Martin's own playing style.

Here is how Martin describes it:

"It is really just old-fashioned baseball. When talent is in short supply, be certain the fundamentals are sound: Never miss a cutoff man, do not botch a rundown. If there is no home run hitter in the lineup, put on the double steal. Bunt to get on base. Hit behind the runner; force the action. In short, simply manufacture something that you might not deserve—a run."

Here is a typical example of what he meant:

In one game against Seattle, Rickey Henderson of the A's led off the first inning with a walk, then stole second base. After one out, he stole third. The pitcher, thoroughly rattled, walked Cliff Johnson, the designated hitter. Johnson, one of the slowest men in baseball at the time, then stole second base because the Seattle catcher was afraid of Henderson's speed on third. Both Henderson and Johnson then scored on Mike Heath's single. Result: two runs on just one hit.

Steal King

If coaches should wonder about the value of having a fine base stealer on the team, they should listen to what Joe Torre, former big league manager, said about his former St. Louis Cardinals teammate Lou Brock, the game's all-time base stealer.

"Lou bothered the infielders just by making them move around and thus play out of position. He messed up the pitchers' timing. They'd look over their shoulders and try to throw the ball to the plate at the same time. Lou especially bothered the young

2. **"Green Light":** This is for an exceptional base runner, who is allowed to steal any time he wishes. However, if a coach figures the opposition has a play on, such as a pitch out, then he can give the sign not to steal, and keep it on until he feels the situation again favors the runner. A good rule in any situation is for a runner not to go unless he can get a good break on the pitch.

DOUBLE STEAL: Normally used with a runner on first and second, or first and third.

1. **First and Second Steals:** Part of what is termed a *straight steal* action. The runner on first base takes a longer lead, and he must key on the runner at second base. If he is sent down, then the runner at first must go for second base to keep the catcher occupied or make at least one part of the play a success.

2. **First and Third Steals:** The objective of this move is twofold: first, to score the runner from third base; and second, to take away the possible double play by getting the runner to second base, even if it keeps the runner from scoring from third. At lower levels, you quite often see the runner from first base giving himself up by getting involved in run-downs.

A variety of things can happen on this play. One, it can be a straight steal, with the runner on first going to second. The runner at third, once the ball crosses the plate, can make a couple of jabs at going home to delay the catcher from throwing the ball, and if there is enough delay, second base can be stolen.

The runner at first base, whether or not the catcher makes a throw, should slide to the outside of the base line so the fielder, in making the tag, will be out of position, and spend a precious second or two setting himself to make a throw to the plate. The runner on third should not head for the plate until he sees the catcher's throw clear the pitcher's head—sometimes the catcher will try to snag him with a throw back to the pitcher, hoping he has made a too hasty break for the plate.

A second variety is a steal when the pitcher begins his stretch motion. An inexperienced pitcher may be so startled that he commits a balk. But what is more likely to happen is the pitcher stepping off to make a play at first base. The first baseman must check the runner at third, then throw to whoever is covering second base. Or the runner may stop and tease the defense into a rundown situation, which often happens at lower levels. In either case, the runner at third will edge down the line toward home and be ready to break if there is a play at second base.

At top levels of competition, the runner will go full blast for second base and the first baseman then is stuck with the decision of how long to check the runner at third and still try for the out at second. If he checks too long, there may be a stolen base; if he gets into a play at second, the runner may be able to steal home.

A third option is called the *long lead,* trying to induce the pitcher to make a play on the runner at first base. The moment he does, the runner breaks for second, and again the first baseman has to make a decision, with the options the same as before.

There can be a definite package of signs for the long-lead situation, distinct and apart from the straight steal, as was illustrated in Chapter 1. Each of them is at a different section of the body, and the options for both are governed by various hand movements on those areas. With the long-lead package, there can be a sign for a straight steal, telling the runner he must break for second as soon as the pitcher throws to first base; a second sign that tells them to stay put if the pitcher does not make a play; and even a third when the pitcher does not make a play and pitches the ball.

We will discuss the sets later in this chapter.

Delayed Steal: Used any time with runners at first and third, with any type of runner. Some situations to look for are: when the coach sees the catcher just lobbing the ball back to the pitcher after each pitch, when the

pitchers who kept hearing 'Lou Brock, Lou Brock,' and then they found out what they kept hearing was true.

"When Lou got on base, a catcher found himself trying to get the ball out of his glove before it even got to him. It soon became a chain of errors. Baseball is a game of rhythm, and when you don't have that rhythm, you wind up standing there watching Lou Brock steal bases."

DELAYED STEAL: Hot sign

second baseman and shortstop are playing deep, or if the second baseman has a habit of looking down after each pitch is past the batter.

It is best to have a fast runner at first base to make this maneuver work in either of two ways. The first way is for the runner at first base to break as soon as the ball crosses the plate. Now, the catcher is forced to "look" the runner on third back to the bag before trying to get the other runner, and the delay can be enough to get the steal of second. The second way starts off the same, except the runner at third makes motions as if he is going to come home, and again the catcher is forced to check his moves, and if he doesn't, the runner at third can steal home.

Some coaches like this maneuver with a young left-handed pitcher. As he comes to his set position, the runner on first takes off, and though the pitcher knows there is a runner on third, his first reaction is getting the man breaking for second, sometimes just by making a motion toward the bag. But the other runner, knowing the play is on, heads for the plate provided the pitcher does not back off the mound.

LONG-LEAD STEAL PACKAGE: Runner should stay if pitcher "picks" at his base

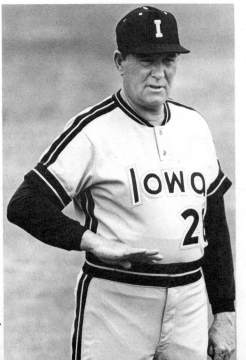

THE SIGNS

There is a special package of signs that can be established to cover the various steal situations. All are dependent upon the talent and how it will be used. For instance, if a coach plans to use only one player as a bona fide threat, he need not install an elaborate package because, depending on the play action, he will always have a "green light," and need only know the "don't steal" sign.

However, if the team makes varied use of the stolen base, then there are four basic signals: the steal, the delayed steal, the double steal, and don't steal, and they are used in the straight steal and long-lead steal packages. In putting together these packages, a coach should lessen any confusion by placing each package at a separate part of the body, and have all the variations of each originate from that location by a simple hand movement.

When we set up our system of signs earlier in the book, you will recall that we placed the *steal* and *delayed steal* signs in Section 3 of our body form; and the *long-lead steal* in Section 4. Both are next to each other, in an area just above the belt and below the shoulders. Therefore, when runners and batters see the coach's hand in those areas, they know immediately there is a steal—nothing else—and he should then zero in on the hand's location to get the precise kind of play.

In Section 3, the *straight steal* can simply be the flat hand resting against the body; the *delayed steal* can be the flat hand with the fingers being rubbed upward. The delayed steal can be worked off the straight steal, or the long-lead steal, and it tells the runner at first base what he is to do.

The *long-lead steal* package in Section 4 can begin with a swipe of the hand across the body telling the runner to go if the pitcher throws, or "picks," at his base; it can be a hand swipe downward if the pitcher doesn't pick, telling him to stay put; and it can be a hand swipe upward if the pitcher throws the ball home without picking at him.

The "suit yourself" sign simply reaffirms the "green light," but I much rather prefer the "don't steal" in my package. If the "suit yourself" sign is desired, it can be something away from the right hip since it is used so infrequently.

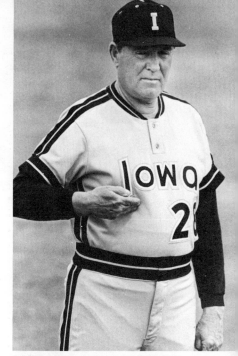

LONG-LEAD STEAL PACKAGE:
Runner should go if pitcher throws home.

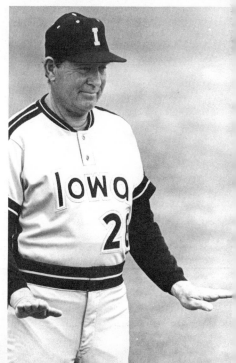

DON'T STEAL/PLAY SAFE.

COACHES' QUIZ

1. Stealing a base should be determined by:

   a. the pitcher
   b. the speed of the runner
   c. catcher's arm
   d. all of the above

2. The basic rule in stealing third base is:

   a. any time
   b. with no outs or two outs
   c. only with a fast runner
   d. all of the above

3. The most important thing in stealing home is:

   a. foot speed
   b. poor catcher
   c. pitcher's poor delivery movements
   d. all of the above

4. The term "green light" gives the runner the:

   a. right to go on his own
   b. keeps the runner under control of coach
   c. forces the runner to steal
   d. all of the above

5. On a first/third situation the runner on third should break:

   a. on the pitch
   b. as soon as the catcher releases the ball
   c. when the ball goes over the pitcher's head
   d. none of the above

CHAPTER 6
SLIDE OR STAND UP, KEEP RUNNING OR STOP RUNNING

Running the bases certainly is an important skill for any player, but how well a player does it often depends on the help that he receives from the first and third base coaches. They are baseball's traffic cops, and during a game they control the activities of the runners with both physical and verbal signals. This, of course, is done in addition to going about their other duties of flashing signs to batters and runners.

Once the ball is hit, the action falls into their laps because they become a second pair of eyes—and in some cases, one very important pair of eyes—for base runners. Their judgments are most important; but even more so is the manner in which they direct that traffic and issue the proper orders to keep it moving—or not moving.

While to the average fan the job as a first or third base coach might not look important, in fact it is very demanding, and sometimes not too secure. Any doubters can talk to Mike Ferraro, once a third base coach for the New York Yankees who was fired after a playoff series several years ago by team owner George Steinbrenner because he sent home a runner who was thrown out on a hairbreadth play at the plate. It was an irrational act on the part of the Yankee owner who was so bitterly disappointed by his team's loss in the playoff series, but it nonetheless pointed to the frailty of the job.

The prime talent both base line coaches must possess is the ability to condense every possible situation, and the talents of as many as thirteen men on the field at the time, into split-second judgments. They must go through a mental check list of options that is more worthy of the fastest

LOOK-TOUCH-LOOK

computer because people are depending upon decisions in a matter of seconds after a ball is hit.

Communication, usually verbal, is the biggest part of their job, so let's look at what each does and what may be the best method for issuing all the signs and signals that keep an offense flowing:

First Base Coach: There are four specific instances when he is called upon to function:

1. With no runners on base, he should stand in the rear end of the coach's box and be aware of all that is happening in the game, as well as watching for some helpful clues around his own area of the field, such as positioning of fielders. He also may be called upon to flash signs to the batter, and to look for tip-offs from the way the catcher gives pitching signs to the pitcher, or how he moves his body on certain pitches.

2. When a runner gets to first base, he must tell him where the ball is, how many outs, what to do on ground balls, long fly balls, or medium fly balls, and remind him about specific strengths of a fielder—any situation, regardless of how elemental. These come under the heading of verbal signs. His position in the coaching box is at the furthest point from home plate where he can coach the runner on getting off the bag, or holding his set position; and watching the pitcher for plays on the runner by reminding him of the pitcher's pickoff move.

3. When he is helping a runner with a base hit, and the ball is in front of the runner, he will tell him so; and if it is not, he'll tell him that, too. Meanwhile, he waves him on with vigorous arm rotations and yells at him to make the turn, so he can see the play in front of him. On balls hit down either foul line, the coach must make a quick judgment whether to keep the runner going to second base.

4. With a runner at first and second, or whenever the first baseman is playing off the bag, and behind the runner, the coach should stand at the home plate side of the box so he clearly can watch the first baseman. On bunt situations with the first baseman playing in front of the runner, he watches the second baseman.

I cannot emphasize too much the importance of the verbal signs. If a first base coach is certain the runner cannot advance on a hit, he should yell, "Make your turn...Hold up!" and if he feels he can make second base—even though the runner can see the play in front of him—he should command him, "Go for two!"

Where there are extreme crowd noises, he should cup his hands in advising his runner of the situation and the options, and tell him whether or not he is the tying or winning run; or if neither, tell him his run isn't decisive, so not to take any chances of becoming a foolish out.

Pulling a Fast One!

Gene Michael, former Yankee manager and general manager and present third base coach, is considered the uncrowned champion of the hidden ball trick.

"I only pulled it five times in my career, but the truth is that I could have done it a lot more times if I'd wanted to. It's always easier to pull it at second base because the runner usually has to do something extra to get there, like hit a double or steal the base. That seems to cause a temporary loss of his concentration.

"But if you keep doing it, you run the risk of antagonizing the player you have fooled. He thinks you are showing him up. The first one I worked was against Zoilo Versalles of the Twins. He said later that I was bush, and I said, 'Why? He was the guy who made the mistake.'"

Why didn't Michaels take advantage of all his opportunities?

"Human nature, I guess. I just didn't want to run the risk of antagonizing people."

Not every coach can be certain he'll meet such a nice guy...so beware, brother. Beware.

THIRD BASE COACH:
Correct position for controlling runner.

Third Base Coach: He has a bit more complexity to his job. He gets the runners coming around the bases so he must make split-second decisions, yet he also cannot forget his duties because he has charge of runners on second and third base. Here, the coach should give him the same kind of information given to the runner at first: number of outs, game situation, and location of the ball. He should tell him how the infield is playing, and on fly balls, whether to tag up, or on short fly balls, whether to drift off third base about fifteen feet. And then he must direct him whether to score on a fly ball, as well as whether to go home on balls hit to the infield.

His other decision-making processes are governed by:

- Base runner's speed and baserunning ability
- Score and inning
- Abilities of following batters
- Defensive talent, including their ability to track down a ball; throwing-arm strength from any area of the field; quickness of a defense's relay from the outfield; and the courage of the catcher to withstand a collision at home plate

In addition, the coach must almost be capable of looking two ways at once—at the runners who are his responsibility, and at the ball in play and what is happening with it.

The runner also has responsibilities concurrent with the coaches. When he can see where balls are hit, the runner often has the option of whether or not to go to third base, particularly at higher levels of competition where he can judge the strength of an outfielder's arm. Sometimes a fielder will loaf in getting to a ball and if the runner picks that up, he often can make an extra base on his own. Or there are some runners, again at higher levels, who can decoy an outfielder into thinking he really isn't going too far, and then when he sees the fielder be nonchalant with the ball, he takes off and gets an extra base.

But any time there is a hit to right field and the runner is coming from first base, he must look for that third base coach even before he gets to second. We call this a look-touch-look sequence: He *looks* at the coach as he starts to make his turn around second base, and the coach will tell him whether to keep coming, then he *touches* the base as he rounds the bend, and then *looks* again for the coach's signal on what to do. It is important for the second look because the third base coach might realize he has made a mistake initially waving the runner around second, and will want him to hold up, and go back.

There are specific situations that concern the third base coach:

THIRD BASE COACH: Correct position for giving signs.

1. ***Runner Coming into Third Base, Standing*** · In all instances, the coach must be visible to the runner, so he should move down the line, toward home plate and away from the third baseman who will be covering the bag. If the coach sees there will be no play on the runner, yet he cannot score, he can point to the bag when the runner is about twenty feet away, giving him time to run under control. A simple "Stand up, hold it there!" backs up the hand signal.

2. ***Runner Must Slide into Third Base:*** Again, the coach frees himself from being hidden yet gets close enough to the bag where the runner can see him. Many coaches will get down on their knees and motion for the runner to slide. I'll go down to one knee and point in the direction I want the runner to slide into the bag and also yell at the runner, "Slide, slide, slide!" and I'll do it as soon as I see it may be necessary. Again, a verbal direction.

What about runners who will score?

When I see that is possible, I'll wind my arm in a rapid-fire series of circular motions and yell at him, "Score, score, score!"

Then there always are instances where the coach is not quite certain whether the runner can make it. Here, I want him to come into third and make the turn, under some control, until I can see for certain what has developed. If he can't go further, I'll point at the bag quickly and yell at him to hold, and go back. If he can score, I'll wave him on, and give the "score, score, score!" yell.

The toughest play is monitoring two runners, say with a man on first and second and a ball is slashed near the gap, or a runner is coming from first base on a possible triple. The lead runner is the first responsibility, so I will go down the line and direct him toward the plate, and then, while also watching the ball in play, hustle back near the bag to get into the vision of the runner coming from first base. Often, if I can see that the lead runner can easily score, I won't even move down the line, but just wave him around, and then concentrate on the action with the ball and the other runner, or with the batter if it appears a hit will become a triple. At that point, the communication is dictated by what will happen with the relay.

RUNNER COMING INTO THIRD BASE SLIDING

RUNNER COMING INTO THIRD BASE STANDING UP

SCORE, SCORE, SCORE!

HOLDING RUNNER AT THIRD

On balls hit to right field, the runner needs help once he reaches second base. In other words, as long as he can see the ball in play, he forms his own judgments, though a coach must also reinforce them—or, in some instances, change them—according to what he sees.

On a ground ball to the right side of the infield, a runner on second base is expected to move up automatically to third base. If it goes into the outfield, he should try to score. If a ground ball is hit with less than two outs to the left side of the infield—to the shortstop or third baseman—the runner on second base is expected to hold up until the ball goes into the outfield. There are exceptions to this rule, but generally the runner must be certain of making it safely to third before setting out. Upon arrival at second base, the runner should look to the third base coach for signals that will remind him what he is to do on balls batted to different parts of the field. Here is a series of signs that can be employed to communicate with the runner.

FLY BALL TO LEFT FIELD

Cute Innovators

Like so many of baseball's innovative offensive maneuvers, the hit-and-run, as well as the run-and-hit, had its genesis with the old Baltimore Orioles of the 1890s where John McGraw and Wee Willie Keeler were two of major league baseball's great innovative players at the time.

McGraw was the Orioles leadoff hitter, and Keeler batted second, and together they worked out a cute play. When McGraw got on, he would fake a steal of second, and Keeler would watch to see whether the second baseman or the shortstop moved to cover the bag.

This, of course, told Keeler where to hit the pitch when McGraw did go for second base, and, as one of the greatest bat control players ever to play in the major leagues, he could punch the ball through the vacant area. McGraw usually made it to third base on the play.

"We used to sit up nights thinking of new plays," McGraw once said of his time with the Orioles.

Those plays soon became commonplace in baseball, and have been an integral part of the game ever since.

Tricks of the Trade

A first and third base coach can take nothing for granted. They must have the eyes of an eagle and an attention span to match if they don't wish to fall prey to some embarrassing moments.

Like the hidden ball trick...or the false rumor.

A great example of the latter occurred in a game at Yankee Stadium several seasons ago when Chicago White Sox rookie Rusty Kuntz broke for second base on a hit-and-run grounder by teammate Alan Bannister, which skimmered down the first base line and out of the rookie's vision.

Yankee first baseman Bob Watson grabbed the grounder in fair territory and tagged out Bannister. He saw Kuntz standing safely on second base, so he tossed the ball back to pitcher Ron Guidry, standing on the pitching mound.

A moment later, Guidry saw Kuntz walking back toward first base, so he whirled and picked him off. Kuntz, it seems, was a victim of a "rumor" from shortstop Fred Stanley, that Bannister's ball had been foul, and automatically began to return to his base.

Kuntz's major error: He didn't ask his coaches for advice, or if he got it, he didn't double check. The coaches' error: They weren't convincing enough—if in fact they even told him to stay put.

...and the hidden ball trick, as old as the game itself.

78

Type of Batted Ball	Action Desired of Runner	Signal
1. Fly ball to left field.	Go halfway and watch play.	Point left hand skyward to left and left centerfield, then cross arms at wrists.
2. Fly ball to centerfield	Tag up and advance to third base.	Point left hand skyward and then draw extended arm toward body.
3. Fly ball to right field.	Tag-up and advance to third base.	Point right hand skyward to right center and right field, then draw extended right hand toward body.
4. Line drive, hit anywhere.	Check to see if it falls safely before advancing.	Jab both arms straight out from body, then point to eyes and extend hand out, palms outward.

FLY BALL TO CENTER FIELD

Type of Batted Ball	Action Desired of Runner	Signal
5. Ground ball to left side of infield.	Advance only if the ball goes into the outfield.	Point to left side of infield with left hand. Make walking fingers motion with right hand and end with right hand passing beyond extended left arm, demonstrating ground ball going through infield into outfield. Then draw extended left arm toward body.
6. Ground ball to right side of infield.	Advance to third base.	Point to right side of infield. Make walking fingers motion with right hand to right side of infield, then draw extended right hand toward body.

FLY BALL TO RIGHT FIELD

Decoding the Message

One good rule for sign stealers is to check to see if you've ever played with someone on the other side of the diamond. He may still be using some familiar signs.

It happened in the 1952 World Series between the Dodgers and Yankees. The Dodgers led the Yankees two games to one, and trailed by only one run in the fourth inning of the fourth game. Brooklyn had runners on second and third, and Dodgers manager Charley Dressen flashed the sign to pitcher Joe Black, the batter, to squeeze home the runner at third.

There was only one problem: His squeeze sign was the same one he had used with the Oakland club of the Pacific Coast League, and on that team was infielder Billy Martin. Martin also was playing second base for the Yankees that day, and he caught the sign and flashed it to catcher Yogi Berra, who called for a pitch low and outside that Black simply could not touch.

The runner at third base never had a chance—and neither did the Dodgers rally, nor their chance to go up 3-1 in that World Series.

LINE DRIVE, HIT ANYWHERE —————————

————— GROUND BALL TO LEFT SIDE OF INFIELD

GROUND BALL TO RIGHT SIDE OF INFIELD

Slide Rule...

Sometimes all the exhortations in the world from a coach to a runner, telling him to "slide, slide, slide," don't do a bit of good.

Hall of Fame manager Casey Stengel told of the time he was managing the Brooklyn Dodgers and his team was playing the New York Giants at the Polo Grounds. Frenchy Bordargaray hit a double, and then he wanted to steal third.

"I wouldn't give him the sign," Stengel recalled. "But when the next batter singled, I waved him home. The ball came off the left field wall, which was shallow at one part of the Polo Grounds, and their left fielder threw it home quickly.

"Now, I figure our Frenchy knows it can be a tough play, but I tell him as he passes me, 'slide, slide, slide.' But I guess he's still mad at me for not lettin' him steal, and he pays no attention.

"So there is their catcher, Gus Mancuso, standing at home plate looking like he's waiting for a trolley car and ol' Frenchy thinks he's got this whole thing figured out and wants to trot across home plate.

"Well, Mr. Mancuso wasn't as dumb as he looked. As soon as Frenchy reached him, he just tagged him out.

"After the game, I said to Frenchy, 'That will cost you twenty-five dollars.'

" 'That was a dumb play,' he told me. 'Better make it fifty.' "

COACHES' QUIZ

1. The key to success in running the bases is:

   a. the hitter
   b. the coaches
   c. the runner
   d. none of the above

2. The prime talent both base line coaches must have is the ability to:

   a. give the signs
   b. argue with umpires
   c. evaluate every possible situation
   d. none of the above

3. The first base coach must:

   a. tell the runner the number of outs
   b. help the runner on a base hit
   c. alert runner to errant throws
   d. all of the above

4. The third base coach:

   a. gives number of outs
   b. gives information as to how infield is playing
   c. determines when runner should score
   d. all of the above

5. Any time there is a hit to right field the runner approaching second base must:

   a. look to third base coach
   b. put his head down and run
   c. look to right field and stop at second base
   d. none of the above

6. The first base coach's toughest task is:

   a. monitoring two runners
   b. making a decision to score a runner
   c. making himself visible to the runner
   d. none of the above

CHAPTER 7

INFIELD/OUTFIELD SIGNALS

Signs and signals in a baseball game are not limited to the offense. Indeed, the necessity of establishing a package for all nine fielders is at least as great because there must be a coordination of efforts to counteract the offense's maneuvers in the various situations that confront a defense. It is the same as in all sports—sound defense pressures offensive players to change what they may do best. But, also as in other sports, a defense is only as good as the execution.

I always make it an integral part of our practice sessions, from day one, to integrate the defensive calls with the signs and signals that we give our hitters and runners. First of all, this tells the team that all three areas are of equal importance, and that we want to work them in together as part of our drills. Therefore, we set up situations with runners on, flash signs to our hitters and runners, and do the same to the defense so it can align itself for that particular situation.

For example, if we are working on the hit-and-run, the batter and the runner will get their signs as if it was a game situation—remember, you play like you practice. But the infielders, outfielders, pitcher, and catcher also will use their defensive signs to cope with the tactic. It is the same with a bunt. The batter and runner will get the signs, but the catcher also will get one that sets up one of our bunt defenses. Over the course of our practices everyone takes a turn in the field and at bat so that all of the various signs and signals will be familiar to starter and substitute alike.

I believe this kind of integrated drill is very meaningful for teams that do not have several coaches or many players because it serves as a check for lead-up drills to implement the full offensive and defensive structure. Everyone works and is tightly focused on one area, and eventually all the situations

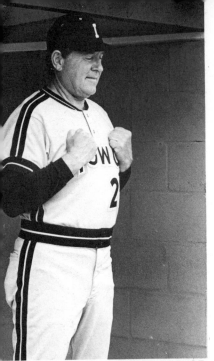

BUNT DEFENSE:
Normal Coverage

that they will face during a game can be covered with a judicious use of practice time.

As with the signs for runners and hitters, we also set up our defensive package in a team meeting, right at the start of our practice term, and we review it constantly throughout the season, regardless of how many times we may be using it. Unlike some of the offensive situations that require definite talents, there are no exceptions for the defense. A sound grounding, helped by repetitive drills, ultimately will mean the team will handle all of these situations, and the required movements, without having to stop and think, "Okay, what do we do here?"

THE IMPORTANCE OF DEFENSE

Unlike some of the offensive situations, which require definite talents, there are no exceptions for the defense. Basically, the defense wants the offense to do what it dictates by its various alignments in bunt coverage, steals, batted balls, and combination plays from outfield to infield to catcher. In so doing, it dares the offense to be error-free in its execution, and an aggressive defense can put extreme pressure on the offense to be error-free. This is not always possible, and even less so if that defense itself is not error-free.

There are six areas to consider when establishing a defense, and then utilizing the signs and signals that help make it run:

1. ***Bunt Defense:*** There are at least three different alignments, but each has several variations which dovetail with different kinds of pickoff action. One that caught my eye occurred in the 1984 World Series, between San Diego and Detroit. The Padres, on one defense, allowed second baseman Alan Wiggins to rush toward the plate to play the bunt, and kept first baseman Steve Garvey close to the bag. Regardless of which might be used, they all must be regulated by the same factors that determine offensive actions: runners on base, score, inning, and the capability of the runner and bunter. The sign usually is flashed by the coach in the dugout to the catcher or the third baseman, who then relays it to the pitcher and infielders. They pass it on to the outfielders. There is one mandate in all this: Keep transmission as simple as possible so the sign does not have to pass through too many people. Establish what sign the catcher or third baseman will use to relay it to the other fielders—it could be a body movement with hands or feet.

a. ***Normal Coverage:*** The sign can be as simple as both fists together on the upper chest, and this can be flashed first with a couple of meaningless signs to follow. The first or third baseman, or the pitcher, will

BUNT DEFENSE: Crash/Funnel-4

handle the bunt in this situation and throw to the second baseman covering first. The catcher will direct the throw, and if the third baseman makes the play, he will move up and cover third base.

b. *Crash/Funnel-4:* This is a good play with runners on first and second, and the coach knows the opposition will be bunting. His sign can be placing the flat of his hand on his right side, just below the belt. The pitcher must acknowledge that sign, perhaps by waggling the top of his glove.

The second baseman cheats a bit toward first base, as he normally does in a sacrifice situation; then with the pitcher in a stretch position, he starts a sprint toward home plate. The pitcher will deliver the ball when he sees the second baseman half way between home and first. The second baseman comes under control from his sprint about halfway between home and first, to be ready to field the bunt.

The pitcher comes off the mound toward the third base line. The third baseman must read whether he can field the bunt. If he sees that the pitcher can make the play, he retreats to the bag; if not, he makes the play to first base. The catcher's directions are important in determining the action of the third baseman.

c. *Sprint-6:* Again, good with a runner on first and second, and the coach knows the opposition will be bunting. He flashes a sign, placing his left hand on his left side, below the belt if he just wishes the team to play the bunt. If he wants the pitcher to work a "pick" off this maneuver, he will pick his pants with that hand.

BUNT DEFENSE: Sprint-6

Here, the pitcher will key on the action of the shortstop, who will take two steps toward second base, hoping to push the runner back toward the bag. He then will pivot and sprint toward third base. When the second baseman sees the shortstop sprinting, he moves to that imaginary line between second and first to take away any slash hit, and then dashes to the first base bag.

Once the pitcher sees the shortstop halfway between the runner and third base on his sprint, he delivers the ball. The first and third basemen will key on the shortstop's split distance, and they will charge hard at the same time, and play the bunt.

Here is an example of a "pick" by the pitcher off a bunt defense: The shortstop takes two steps beyond the runner at second to chase him back, and the second baseman takes one step toward first. As soon as the second baseman sees the shortstop even with the runner at second, he sprints to the bag. The pitcher, in a stretch position, watches until the shortstop is two or three steps beyond the runner (the runner will probably start his lead again), and then he will turn and throw the ball to the second baseman, who by this time has reached the bag.

PICK-OFF BUNT DEFENSE

Musial Caged

Then there was Birdie Tebbetts's four-man outfield—he placed the third baseman in the outfield whenever Stan Musial of St. Louis was the hitter and the Cardinals needed an extra-base hit to win the game against his Cincinnati Reds team.

That was a reverse of the five-man infield that Branch Rickey is credited with originating with the Cardinals. He stationed an outfielder between the pitcher and the first baseman whenever a poor hitter was at bat—but only in two situations: with a runner on first and a sacrifice upcoming, the extra man fielded the bunt and the first baseman held the runner close; or if a runner was at third, there was an extra chance of cutting him down at the plate if he hit a ground ball.

2. *Batted Ball Defense:* When the defense feels this play is coming, the coverage becomes a bit of a cat-and-mouse game with the offense. Will the second baseman move to cover the bag? Or will he stay put and allow the shortstop to cover? If he stays put, then a batter's attempt to hit behind the runner into right field can become a double play. If he doesn't, it may become a hit. But who's to know?

The shortstop and second baseman will know because after every pitch, they should use the "open mouth–closed mouth" signal system. Shielding their faces behind their gloves, they look at each other, and the man—usually the shortstop—who gives the "open mouth" sign is saying—without saying a word— "I'm telling you to cover the bag." Or it can be the other way around—if the mouth is closed, the shortstop takes the bag.

3. *Steal Situation, with Hit-and-Run, Run-and-Hit Possibility:* The open mouth–closed mouth signal system is used when the defense senses there might be a steal. The defense still must keep the offense guessing as to what its coverage will be, regardless of whether the batter is right-handed or left-handed. If the defense does fool the offense in gunning down one of those plays, then the next time the offense may go away from its strategy. If so, consider it a win for the defense.

4. *Comebacker to Pitcher:* With a man on first base, the shortstop and second baseman again must have a signal as to which of them will cover second base when a ball is hit back to the pitcher, because he obviously will

SHORTSTOP-SECOND BASEMAN SIGNALS: Open mouth-closed mouth syste

be trying to start a double play. Either the shortstop or second baseman will flash the signal to the pitcher to enable him to make his throw, usually to the shortstop because his momentum is going toward the bag. An exception would be if the shortstop is playing slightly out of position; then the second baseman would cover.

Normally, with a left-handed batter at the plate, the pitcher would look for the shortstop to take the throw, but if the defense aligns itself where the second baseman is close to the bag, the pitcher must get a signal from him that he will be covering the bag, and thus be prepared to aim his throw accordingly.

This kind of alignment happens often at lower levels of competition where the coach controls his defensive setup, but the pitcher still must know who will get his throw. At higher levels, where fielders are set pretty much by hitting tendencies and types of pitches, much of this will be automatic because fielders will shift with each pitch, and so will their responsibilities.

5. **Positioning Outfielders According to the Pitch:** There are no hard and fast rules any more about positioning outfielders because many coaches prefer to make decisions based on hitters' tendencies. However, at all times they will consider the outfielder's ability to go back on the ball, his arm strength, and the depth a hitter usually will hit the ball. But for those who feel it useful, the signs are made from the infielder to the outfielder. Sometimes they will use finger flashes behind their back—one finger for a fast ball, two for a curve; others will use closed fist for a fast ball, open hand is

I'VE GOT (THE THROW TO 2ND BASE ON A) COMEBACKER TO PITCHER

INFIELDER-OUTFIELDER SIGNALS: Open fist for curve ball; closed fist for fast ball.

Closing the Gaps

Here are nine basic factors that a coach should consider as a part of his philosophy on:

(1) Whether the team is home or away
(2) The score
(3) The inning
(4) The situation with outs and men on base
(5) Upcoming hitters and skills of each
(6) Baserunning skills of men on base and upcoming hitters for each particular situation
(7) Bench players available for pinch-hitting and pinchrunning
(8) Your pitcher's fatigue factor
(9) Opposing pitcher's fatigue and control

Shifting infielders and outfielders to compensate for certain hitting tendencies has taken some radical turns at times.

a curve ball. The danger is that too quick a move to the right by the shortstop before the pitch can tip the hitter that there may be a curve ball coming.

6. ***Relay and Cutoff Calls:*** These signals are verbal. We must consider the duties of four individuals—relay man, trailer, cutoff man, and the catcher. When a ball is hit beyond the outfielder, in left center field, for example, the shortstop is the relay man who will go out to relay the outfielder's throw back to the infield. Since he is watching the outfielder and awaiting his throw, he does not get a look at the base runners. But the second baseman should go with him as a "trailer," and stay approximately twenty feet behind him to tell him where to throw the ball and back him up in case there is an errant throw by the outfielder.

The trailer sees the action and tells the relay man the precise direction, yelling, "Third, third, third," or "Home, home, home."

The cutoff man and catcher then get into the act, with the catcher controlling the action once the ball has left the relay man, to make what I consider one of the most difficult plays in baseball because he must judge several things at once: Can the runner score? Is the relay action precise enough to make a play at the plate? Is the relay man's arm strong enough to get the runner from the spot where he catches the ball in relation to the runner's distance from home? Is the other base runner or hitter fast or alert enough to take an extra base on the play and thus set up another possible run-scoring situation?

If the catcher feels that the ball coming from the relay man can reach him in time to make a play, he will not say a word, and allow it to come through. But if he wants the cutoff man, who should be in a direct line between him and relay man, to handle it and stop all baserunning action, he

INFIELD BACK

INFIELD IN

yells, "Cut, cut, cut!" If he wants him to make a play on a base runner, he yells his directions as to which base the ball must be thrown, such as, "Cut two, cut two!" telling him to cut off the ball and throw it to second base; or if he sees a sudden chance for a play at the plate, "Cut four, cut four!" meaning the cutoff man is to throw the ball home.

These fielders can decoy to their benefit while this is going on, too. The cutoff man can feign a catch to make a runner break his stride, or stop altogether, and perhaps get a play on him when he does get the ball.

And don't forget the role of the pitcher during all of this action: He must be certain to back up third base if there is a chance the throw will be coming there from right field, or back up the catcher if it appears there will be a play at the plate. If he is not sure, he will split the distance and wait to see what happens before moving behind third or home.

POSITIONING OF INFIELDERS

There are three basic moves here, and all signs come from the coach:

1. *Infield Back:* The almost universal sign is for the coach to push both his palms in the direction of the infielders, placing them at normal depth.

2. *Infield In:* The infielders are set at an imaginary base line that runs between first and second, and second and third, or at the edge of the infield grass. The coach simply turns both palms inward and pulls them toward his body. This is not good strategy in the early innings and there are some

One of the most famous in the immediate post–World War II era was the Boudreau shift, named after Cleveland Indians shortstop-manager Lou Boudreau, which he used whenever his team played against Ted Williams of the Red Sox.

Williams, perhaps the greatest left-handed hitter of the post–Babe Ruth era, blistered the right field and right center field portions of the diamond.

So Boudreau placed himself just to the second base side of the bag, moved second baseman Joe Gordon midway between first and second and back near the outfield grass, and pushed first baseman Luke Easter close to the foul line. Third baseman Al Rosen moved closer to the shortstop position as the only infielder on that side of the diamond. Boudreau also shifted his outfielders radically toward right field.

COVER THE CORNERS

INFIELD, PLAY HALFWAY

The genesis of that radical idea came after a game in 1948 when Boudreau became the first player since 1889 to get five extra base hits in one game—only to see his Indians team lose 11-10 on Williams' three homers.

"I was so damn mad at seeing my hits wasted," Boudreau admitted, "that I came up with that cockeyed Williams shift on the spur of the moment. I knew he could pop short flies to left for doubles all day long, but I was willing to take that chance as long as somebody else had to drive him in. Massing the team toward right field worked swell for a long time and everyone copied the shift. But Williams smartened up and began murdering us by hitting to left field every time we shifted on him."

coaches who do not like it at any time, fearing that a grounder will get through the infield; or that a blooper will drop beyond the range of the infielder and in front of the outfielder—but catchable if the infielder was playing at normal depth; or they will do it only in the late innings to give up the tieing run, but in the hopes of keeping the winning run off base.

3. **Infield Halfway:** The corners—first and third basemen—come in while the middle infielders stay back to try to work the double play. A coach usually will fold his arms or cross them in front of his body as the sign for this positioning.

There also are decoy plays which are ideal for lower levels, and these signs also are flashed by the coach. If he drops his hands downward with the wrists facing out, with none or one out and a runner on third base, or with runners at second and third, it means he wants to keep his middle fielders back until the pitch is thrown, when they come up. If the ball is hit on the ground, they are in a position to throw out the runner going home, because he may not have seen them adjust their position, and he would automatically go home on any balls hit to the middle.

Then there is a *reverse play,* the sign for this being the dropping of the hands downward with the wrists pointing toward his body. Here, the middle infielders play in, but at the pitch drop back a few steps. The runner at third knows that with the infield in, he will not try to score on a ground ball and if he does not catch the infielders' move backward, then he might automatically hold third base. The infielder can get an out on the grounder and still keep the run from scoring.

Of course, all of this must be contingent on all of the decision factors we mentioned earlier.

MIDDLE INFIELDERS DROP <u>BACK</u> WHEN PITCH IS THROWN

MIDDLE INFIELDERS COME <u>IN</u> WHEN PITCH IS THROWN

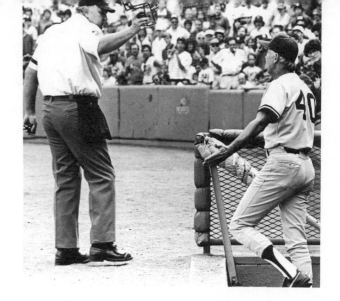

COACHES' QUIZ

1. Defensive signals are:

   a. as important as offensive signals
   b. not important
   c. of questionable value
   d. none of the above

2. The _____ will receive a sign to set the defense for the bunt.

   a. pitcher
   b. shortstop
   c. catcher
   d. none of the above

3. For teams that do not have several coaches _____ is very practical.

   a. separate drills
   b. no drills
   c. integrated drills
   d. none of the above

4. Exceptional talent is _____ for defensive drills.

   a. needed
   b. not needed

5. The most common signal for coverage on the hit-and-run is:

   a. system of numbers
   b. open mouth–closed mouth
   c. system of body touches
   d. none of the above

6. The _____ determine who will cover on a comebacker to the pitcher.

   a. pitcher
   b. catcher
   c. shortstop
   d. none of the above

7. Many coaches no longer give signals to outfielders as to the pitch; they now:

   a. use a system of guesswork
   b. depend on the pitcher
   c. judge hitter tendencies
   d. none of the above

8. On a base hit to the left center _____ is the cutoff man.

   a. the second baseman
   b. the shortstop
   c. the third baseman
   d. none of the above

9. On a base hit to left center the _____ is the trailer.

   a. second baseman
   b. shortstop
   c. third baseman
   d. none of the above

CHAPTER 8
INFIELD PICKOFFS AND DOUBLE STEALS

Some of the most intricate maneuvers on a baseball diamond concern the teamwork and timing that must occur if a team utilizes pickoff plays and special maneuvers to defense double steals.

Anywhere from two to nine players can be involved in some of these plays, particularly when outfielders are in backup positions. So it takes total concentration and coordination to make them work. Of course, a player or coach can't stand out on the field and yell to his players that he wants this or that pickoff play, or defense, against the double steal. Instead, all of these are started from special signs that the team will have as part of its defensive package, though there will be no need for an indicator to set them in motion. It will, instead, be up to the coach to call the plays at each level.

Just as important is the *recognition signal,* which tells the catcher, on most occasions, that his play is on, and everyone is clued in to the process. You can just imagine the chagrin if the first baseman saw the pickoff signal for the runner on his base, and when he rushed over on a timing play to cover the bag, the pitcher delivered the ball and the batter whacked it through the area he had just vacated; or the reverse, where the first baseman did not see the sign and the pitcher, without a close look, threw the ball to the bag and no one covered. I've seen that one happen on all levels of competition, including in the major leagues.

TYPES OF PICKOFFS

There are three types of pickoff plays most commonly used by teams at all levels. They are:

1. **Straight Pick:** This is a "count" play between the shortstop or first baseman, and the pitcher. The infielder must flash the sign because the pitcher has enough to think about without wondering when to institute such an intricate play. However, the pitcher must acknowledge the sign. I know at some lower levels the coach may signal the play to the catcher who then flashes a sign to the infielder to signal the pitcher. But I believe that if a team works on a pickoff system in practice, then the players who are most involved should make the calls—the player who is going to throw the ball and the player who is going to catch it.

The pitcher then takes his stand on the rubber. He looks at the shortstop and then looks at the catcher. His count begins as soon as he turns his head to look at the catcher—1-2-3. The infielder starts to move as soon as the pitcher turns his head to look at the catcher. When the pitcher hits "3," he whirls and throws the ball. Sometimes, this play can be worked by having the catcher drop his glove—at the count of 3—to signal the pitcher to wheel and throw to second base.

2. **Daylight Pick:** Used with a runner on second base. Here, we will allow the shortstop to make the sign. The pitcher must first spot daylight between the shortstop's right knee and the base runner taking a lead toward third base. If the shortstop extends his glove straight out, then he wants the

PITCHER PICKOFF ACKNOWLEDGMENT SIGN

INFIELDER PICKOFF ACKNOWLEDGMENT SIGN

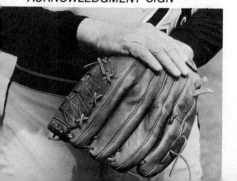

PICKOFF THROW TO SECOND BASE: *Catcher signals to pitcher.*

DAYLIGHT PICK: Shortstop makes sign

pick. The pitcher makes his stretch move, and he can throw to the shortstop, who has broken for the base, if he still sees the shortstop's glove extended. But if the runner has beaten a hasty retreat toward second when he sees the shortstop move, both pitcher and shortstop can call off the play. The pitcher should then wait until the shortstop is at his position before delivering the pitch.

3. *Reverse Turn or Inside Move:* A good maneuver any time with runners at first and second, or just a runner on second. The pitcher works with the shortstop on this play, therefore there must be a sign between them. A right-handed pitcher will raise his knee and turn clockwise (counter-clockwise for a left-hander) toward second base by pivoting on his right foot, with the lead leg pointed at second base. At that point, he throws to the shortstop covering the bag.

4. *Pitcher Fake Pick at Third Base:* This can be executed with runners on first and third base, and is best called on a 3-and-2 count, with two out. It requires a sign between the pitcher and third baseman, and must be acknowledged. The pitcher works from his stretch move, and when he raises his front foot off the ground, the third baseman moves to the bag, and the first baseman takes one or two steps laterally off his bag, where he has been

PITCHER PICKOFF ACKNOWLEDGMENT SIGN TO INFIELDERS

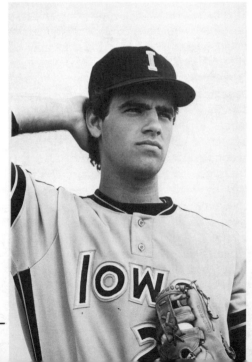

holding the runner. The pitcher then steps off with his left foot toward third base and makes a fake pick motion there. The first instinct of the runner at first base then may be to break for second base. The pitcher, on the fake throw, will plant his right foot toward third base, and turn quickly to his right, reading what the runner at first base is doing. If he sees him running, he will throw to the second baseman, who moves to the short cutoff position, or to the first baseman at the bag—depending on the runner's action—and a rundown can ensue.

Let's look at some situations and how the pickoff play would work in these instances, including the signs that could be used:

1. *Runners on First and Second Base and a Possible Bunt/Steal Situation:* With a right-handed pitcher, the catcher will signal the play to both the pitcher and the first baseman. The pitcher must acknowledge, perhaps by tugging at his left armpit; and so must the first baseman, perhaps by a motion down his gloved arm. The pitcher then steps on the rubber, comes to a set position in his stretch motion and rests his head on his right, or front, shoulder. The first baseman makes it appear as if he will charge the plate to play the bunt, but as soon as he sees the pitcher rest his head on his shoulder, he makes a reverse move backward to the bag as the pitcher makes his throw on the pickoff. The shortstop must hold the runner at second, while the third baseman comes up two steps in a feint to the plate, and reverses to cover third in case the runner at second tries to break.

2. *Runners on First and Second Base, or Man on First Base Only:* This can dovetail with one of the several special bunt defenses. The second baseman will initiate the play with a sign, perhaps his left hand wiggling against his left thigh, and the catcher will acknowledge with a swipe down his left arm. Both the first and third basemen are close to their bases, with the former either holding the runner or in two steps toward the plate. The second baseman will quickly move toward the plate and after he passes an imaginary straight line between the pitcher and first base, the first baseman will quickly retreat to the bag and take a pickoff throw from the pitcher. The third baseman, who is up two steps from the imaginary straight line between second and third bases, scurries back to cover third, and the shortstop fakes the runner back to second base. The outfielders will have been alerted to the play by behind-the-back finger signals from the shortstop and second baseman and then back up the bases in case of an overthrow. Thus, there is a set of multiple signs to make that play possible.

3. *With Runners on First and Second Base, and a Non-Timed Pickoff Play:* The catcher flashes the sign perhaps by wiggling his right hand on his right thigh; the second baseman acknowledges by putting his gloved hand behind his back; and the pitcher acknowledges by wiping his left hand

Running Nightmare

Former clown prince Al Schacht recalled some of the perplexities of the third base coach's job—and why it can be Ulcer City.

"One of our guys tripled with none out and the next batter hit a long fly ball. As soon as the ball hit the outfielder's glove, I yelled 'Go!'

"As the ball was being thrown in, the runner turned to me and said, 'Did you say, "go?"'

" 'Certainly I did,' I told him.

" 'Oh, I thought you said, "Whoa."'

"I went through things like that for thirteen seasons and every night my dreams would always be the same: I'd have two runners winding up on the same base and a mob would be pouring out of the stands to chase me out of the park. I'd wake up exhausted from running.

"Then it came to me. I was getting old before my time because the mob kept getting closer and closer to catching me. That's when I quit and decided to be a clown."

Winning Flash

Leo Durocher was a manager who never let the conventional way of doing things boggle his mind.

In the 1951 World Series, when he was managing the New York Giants against the favored New York Yankees, he came out firing in the opening game. The day before his team had just beaten the Brooklyn Dodgers in the National League playoffs on Bobby Thomson's famous "shot heard 'round the world" home run, and the Giants took right up against the Yankees.

In the first inning of game one, they had a run in, men on second and third with two out, and Thomson at bat. Yankees pitcher Allie Reynolds certainly knew what had happened on Thomson's last at bat; but then Thomson also knew what happened the last time Reynolds had worked. He had pitched his second no-hitter of the 1951 season.

But this time, Reynolds was having problems with his control, and everyone felt the Giants had a chance to put the game away in that first inning with the power-hitting Thomson at bat. Certainly, it was no time to get fancy.

down his right arm. The shortstop breaks toward second base, in front of or behind the runner, and then moves toward third base as if the play has ended. On the shortstop's first stride toward third, the second baseman breaks toward second, and on the shortstop's second stride toward third, the pitcher whirls and throws the ball to the second baseman who will have reached the bag to make a play on the runner. The third baseman takes three steps toward home, and then reverses back to the bag, while the first baseman breaks two steps toward home and reverses back to cover the base.

DEFENSING DOUBLE STEALS

There are four basic plays to defense the double steal—and in these instances we are talking mainly about runners on first and third base.

1. *The Catcher Throws on Through to the Second Baseman:* This happens differently at the higher and lower levels of competition. In the higher levels of professional baseball, where all the players have excellent throwing arms, a catcher often can nab the runner going into second base, and the return throw from either the second baseman or shortstop can also get the

DEFENSING DOUBLE STEAL: Catcher mimicks coach's sign for throw through second base.

runner trying to steal home. In the lower levels, the object is to score the run, so the runner will break for home once he sees the ball sail past the pitcher's head. The sign can be the coach touching his nose and the catcher and infielder mimicking that motion.

In this defense, the catcher's throw must go over the pitcher's head and to the infielder covering second so he can relay it right back to the catcher and either get the runner from third base at home, or begin a rundown with the runner from first base. If the middle fielder can make a play at second, and still get the runner going home, then he's made a major league play. But the first concentration, if there are less than two outs, should be at home plate.

2. **With the Winning Run at Third Base in the Late Innings:** There must be a sign between the catcher and the pitcher, followed by an acknowledge sign, that they don't consider the runner at first base that important, and will concentrate instead in clipping that possible winning run.

The catcher's sign could be a tug at his left ear, and the acknowledge sign could be a touch of the neck. But the acknowledgment is important because the catcher's throw will go to the pitcher. It must be head high to give the illusion to the runner at third that the ball is going through. Runners are

To everyone but Durocher, maybe. Leo had noticed that Reynolds was bearing down so much on Thomson that he was allowing Monte Irvin to take a huge lead off third base. Durocher didn't hesitate—he flashed the steal sign, and in an instant, Irvin stole home, the first player to do so in thirty years in the World Series.

Oh yes. Thomson did not get a hit—and Irvin's run turned out to be the winner.

EFENSING DOUBLE STEAL: Catcher mimicks coach's sign for throw back to tcher.

DEFENSING DOUBLE STEAL: Catcher signals for infielder to be cutoff man.

taught not to take off in such situations unless the ball is at least head high, certainly never at chest height. If the runner falls for the illusion, then the pitcher may have the eager runner trapped off third base.

3. *The Head Knocker:* This is an ideal example of an illusion on the base paths. Base runners at third base always are instructed to come right onto the base line so they can take away the catcher's perspective of just how far they are from the bag. Catchers often will look the man back to the bag, but in the "head knocker," the third baseman will flip his hands up and the catcher will gun the ball to the third baseman, but on a direct line at the base runner's head. The runner's first instinct will be to duck, or even to hit the ground, and if he does, then the defense has him immobile and caught off third base.

4. *Cutoff Catcher's Throw by an Infielder:* Again, the catcher will give the illusion that, with men on first and third, he is trying to get the man stealing second by whipping the ball past the pitcher. The runner on third will break as soon as he sees it pass the pitcher's head, but he may not see the second baseman cut onto the area of the imaginary base line between second and third, and he will be ten to fifteen feet from second base when he catches it and throws it right back to the catcher for a play at the plate. If the second baseman is to take the throw, the sign can be the coach folding his left hand atop his right; and it can be reversed if the shortstop is to get the throw. The catcher may confirm this signal by tossing dirt in the direction—either left or right—of the player who is designated to make the cutoff.

SIGNS FOR DEFENSING DOUBLE STEALS

The coach controls it all because he has a better view of what the runner on third base is doing, perhaps taking too much of a lead, or becoming a bit too antsy or a little careless on how he pays attention to the bag. These are things the players might miss, but if I see them, I want to take advantage of the situation.

Some coaches construct an entire block system for those plays. It may simply mirror the field, with plays by the third baseman starting on the lower left side of the body, the shortstop touching the upper left, the second baseman at the upper right, and first baseman the lower right. For throws to go on through, there is a hand swipe down the middle of the body.

Regardless, a team still must set up its particular package for these situations, and then follow the philosophy that is most easily adaptable by its players. As with the other areas of baseball, they should be part of all the drills and reviewed periodically from the start of the training season.

COACHES' QUIZ

1. The _____ is the quarterback on the field.

    a. pitcher
    b. catcher
    c. shortstop
    d. second baseman

2. The straight pick is a count play between the:

    a. shortstop, second baseman, pitcher
    b. shortstop, second baseman, catcher
    c. shortstop, first baseman, pitcher
    d. none of the above

3. The count play is between:

    a. pitcher and infielder
    b. pitcher and catcher
    c. catcher and infielder
    d. none of the above

4. The key to the daylight play is the pitcher seeing:

    a. daylight between the base and infielder
    b. daylight between the base and runner
    c. daylight between the shortstop's right knee and the base runner
    d. daylight between the shortstop's left knee and the runner

5. The most important part of the play when throwing straight through is:

    a. the pitcher to the catcher
    b. the catcher's throw to second over the pitcher's head
    c. the infielder's position covering the bag
    d. none of the above

6. The "head knocker" is an example of a(n) _____ on the base paths.

    a. bad base runner
    b. illusion
    c. good base runner
    d. none of the above

7. The key in having the second baseman cover is:

    a. he is a better athlete than the shortstop
    b. he is in better position to throw than the shortstop
    c. neither of the above

8. The simplest form of signals for defensive signs is to:

    a. mirror the field
    b. show "hot areas"
    c. use "open mouth–closed mouth"
    d. none of the above

CHAPTER 9
PITCHING SIGNS

The pitcher and catcher may never speak to each other during nine innings of play, but the catcher has a way of speaking volumes as he directs the pitcher's actions—as well as those of his infielders and outfielders—with motions by his fingers, hands, and catching mitt.

Most prominent is the catcher's signaling which pitches he wants the pitcher to throw. Of course, both men have discussed their pitching strategy before the game and they should know the weaknesses and strengths of every hitter. There are some hitters, though, who may not be able to handle the sharp breaking pitch by a flame-throwing pitcher, but yet are dangerous against this same kind of pitch when thrown by a junk-baller. So the strategy must be plotted according to the type of pitcher. But if a catcher and pitcher work together all the time, there is almost a telepathy between them in knowing just which pitch is most effective in every situation, and rarely does the pitcher shake off the catcher's first sign and ask for another.

On the other hand, there are pitchers who will, either because they do not work with the catcher too often or because they insist on plotting their own strategy as the game progresses, shake off one sign after another. The game is, after all, the pitcher's to win or lose, but I am not too impressed with a player who puts his own record over that of his team's. If pitcher and catcher have a problem during the game as to what pitches are being called, then they had better straighten it out, with the coach, between innings.

Several years ago, catcher Carlton Fisk and left-handed pitcher Bill Lee, then teammates on the Boston Red Sox, had a problem with each other during a game. Fisk, who certainly was one of the game's best catchers during the '70s and early '80s, couldn't please Lee with his selection of pitches that day, and was constantly being shaken off. Finally, more out of exasperation than anything else, Fisk marched out to the mound to try to get matters straight with Lee, who tried to build a reputation for being "different." The two talked and soon their conversation became very animated; this

Team Mates

How important do pitchers consider having one catcher work with them all the time?

Steve Carlton, the Phillies' four-time Cy Young Award winner, would work with no other catcher except Tim McCarver when the latter was his teammate on the Phils, and before that, with the St. Louis Cardinals. In fact, at Carlton's insistence, the Phils worked a trade with the Cardinals in order to obtain McCarver and make their star left-handed pitcher a happy man.

"When we die," noted McCarver, "Steve and I will be buried sixty feet, six inches from each other."

(That happens to be the distance the pitching mound is from the catcher's box.)

Sometimes changing pitching signs can be an emotional experience.

In 1956, the Dodgers barnstormed Japan in the fall, and one afternoon while playing the Yomiuri Giants, they were tied 4-4 in the 11th inning. Jackie Robinson was the scheduled hitter and Japanese manager Nobuyasu Mizuhara ordered pitcher Takehito Bessho to walk him intentionally.

But Bessho shook off the catcher's intentional pass sign, so the catcher strode to the mound to get matters straight. Still, the pitcher refused and the frustrated catcher then ran to his dugout and talked to Mizuhara for further instructions. Back he ran to the mound with fresh orders, but to no avail. Bessho still refused to walk Robinson.

Seeing the situation was hopeless, the catcher returned to his post and on the first pitch, Robinson doubled home the winning run.

The manager is usually right—in any language.

animation then moved up to some chest pointing, then to a full-scale shouting match—and all because they couldn't agree on a pitching plan with appropriate signs.

Certainly, I'm not predicting anything so dire, but it at least points out that this can become a very sensitive area unless the two players can agree on their pattern. So the first rule is to be sure both players understand each other before the game begins and encourage them to talk between innings to be sure their pitching game plan still is intact.

GIVING SIGNALS TO THE PITCHER

A catcher's signs for different pitches are almost always given from a squatting position, by means of the fingers. His knees should be close enough together and at such an angle as to make it impossible for the opposing first and third base coaches to see his signals.

The key to the signs is simplicity, and the four basic ones are: *one finger* for a fast ball; *two fingers* for a curve; *three fingers* for a slider; and

FASTBALL

CURVE BALL

SLIDER

four fingers for a special pitch such as a knuckle ball, split-finger fast ball, sinker ball, palm ball, etc. There also are signs that the catcher uses to indicate the location of the pitch, and he normally will do this with a hand position between his legs. For example, if he wants the pitch thrown to the inside of the plate, he will touch the palm of his right hand inside his right thigh. If he wants it thrown outside, he will switch over and touch the thigh of his other leg. If he wants it up and in, he turns his palm toward the pitcher and flicks the fingers upward.

My good friend Bus Campbell, who is one of the most respected pitching coaches in the country and who has tutored over a dozen pitchers currently in the major leagues, has a system that can denote both pitch and location. His pitch signs will be normal—one finger for fast ball, two for curves, etc.—but for location, he divides the upper part of the batter's body into four zones, and gives each a numerical designation, 1 through 4. Number 1 zone calls for a pitch to the outer half of the plate, number 2 to the inside, number 3 is up and inside, and number 4 is down the middle.

He then puts the numerical signs for both the pitch and location together, and adds a decoy system that the pitcher uses all the time so he will

SPECIAL PITCH: Change-up, knuckle ball, palm ball, sinker, etc.

PITCH-OUT SIGN

Basic Fury

Catching a runner trying to steal second base certainly is a boon to a catcher's ego, to say nothing of how it helps his team.

But unless it is carried out to finality, the process also can be a bit deflating.

Take the case of Honus Wagner, the great Hall of Fame shortstop of the Pittsburgh Pirates in the early twentieth century. In St. Louis, one hot, sultry day, with the temperature over 100 degrees, the Pirates were playing the Cardinals and Wagner was on first base. His manager, Fred Clarke, gave him the sign to steal. But the batter swung and missed, and Wagner suddenly found himself hung up between first and second base.

He didn't wait for the first and second basemen to run him down. He just stopped dead, wiped his forehead, and told John Farrell, the Cardinals' first baseman, who had the ball, "I'm not going to let you chase me up and down the base line on a hot day like this," and he just walked away toward first base.

As he did the first baseman threw the ball back to the pitcher, but when Wagner reached first base, instead of going to the dugout, he just stood there.

not have to change if there is a runner on base. It gives him less to think about, and helps him establish his system and keep it going throughout the game. Here is how it could work:

The catcher's first sign is the pitcher's location, the second is a decoy, the third is the pitch itself, the fourth is a decoy, and the fifth is a decoy. Translated into signs by the catcher, it would be 1-2-4-2-2, which the pitcher reads to mean a fast ball down the middle. He knows that only the first and third signs mean anything, and regardless of how many fingers the catcher flashes in the second, fourth, and fifth flashes, they mean nothing.

DANGER TIMES

The ideal situation, of course, is for the pitcher and catcher to walk out on the field and work without a hitch for an entire game. But no one ever said a baseball game is an ideal situation, so there are times when those finger signals may need changing, or at least rearranging if that is the coach's

COMBINATION PITCH AND LOCATION SIGN: In this case, one finger shows fast ball; hand position shows right side of plate (as pitcher faces).

way of fooling the opposition. I call them "danger times," and there are four of which the pitcher and the catcher should be aware:

1. If the catcher is not careful in how he gives the signs, they can be stolen by opposing base line coaches. The first and third basemen should check to see that they are not visible. If so, the player must tell the catcher so he can tighten up, and he simply turns his heels outward in the crouch position and this automatically brings his knees closer together.

2. The movements of the shortstop and second baseman also can tip off the pitches that the catcher calls, simply by the direction in which they move before each pitch.

3. The catcher himself can tip off the pitches by his own mannerisms, such as the way he pumps his arm; the manner in which he moves his feet to receive a certain pitch; and the position of his glove after he has called for the pitch, yet before the pitcher has thrown the ball. Each tip, if picked up, can be signaled to the batter.

4. Possibly, with a runner on first base, and certainly with a runner on second, his signs are more visible. With the runner on first, a catcher can tighten up when giving his signs and prevent the opposition from peeking. A runner on second base has a clear view right to home plate, and like a human camera, his eyes are recording everything he sees. By using his own team's prearranged signs, he can signal the batter what is being called.

So the next move is up to the pitcher and catcher. But any time they change signs, certainly at lower levels, they should try to do so with a meeting on the mound so as not to cross up one another. At higher levels, experienced pitchers and catchers work immediately from a sign signaling the change, with an appropriate acknowledge sign. The key in either case is to be certain both players understand what has been called. We will look at this in greater detail later in this chapter.

SHAKING OFF SIGNS

More often than not in some part of a game, the pitcher will not want to throw the pitch that has been called. He should ask for another, either by rubbing his glove across his shirt, or swiping it down his left side. Now, if the pitcher wants to throw a pitch of his choice, he can use a system whereby he swipes his glove down his side a definite number of times. That number, when added to the number previously flashed by the catcher, will be the pitch he wants to throw.

For instance, if the catcher flashes one finger for a fastball and the pitcher feels that an off-speed pitch, a three-finger sign, would be more

Suddenly, the Cards first baseman realized he had neglected to tag Wagner, and that he was safe on the bag. Furious, he pushed Wagner off the bag, and kept pushing him off, while demanding that the pitcher throw the ball to him. When he got it, he again kept pushing Wagner, tagging him wildly with the ball... all to no avail, of course. Finally, it took all of the umpires and half of the players to subdue him.

Clowning Glory

The late Al Schacht was known as the "Clown Prince of Baseball" because he traveled around the nation and entertained crowds with his zany baseball antics.

But long before his clown act, Schacht was a respected major league third baseman, and for thirteen years, the third base coach for the Washington Senators and Boston Red Sox. Here is how he once described the role of the third base coach:

"It is one of the most responsible positions on a team. Poor judgment on his part can wreck a game. He is in the unenviable position of directing the scoring. If the runner scores, the coach listens to the crowd cheer the player for his speed. If he is cut down at the plate, the coach is blamed.

"Take the first inning. Your leadoff man gets on base. The next batter doubles. You try to score the man from first and he's thrown out on a great play. The third hitter singles and the fourth hits into a double play. You've got one run where you should have had two, and kept the rally going.

effective, he swipes his glove across his shirt to indicate he doesn't want to throw that pitch. The catcher then sees him make two swipes across his chest, and knows to add two to his original sign, and then flashes three fingers for the off-speed pitch.

CHANGING SIGNS

At any level, the signs can change simply by having the catcher make a signal, perhaps by the position of his glove, or as I noted before, with a conference on the mound if there is uncertainty. The pitcher then must signal that he acknowledges the change if it is done only by signal, and the process doesn't end there, because infielders must be aware of the change so they can make their adjustments.

But there are some changes that I believe are very effective for higher levels of competition, and which are difficult for a base runner to decipher. One of these is the *odd-even inning system,* by which the catcher will rotate the finger signs. For instance, in the odd-numbered innings, they can be *one,* fast ball; *two,* curve; *three,* slider; *four,* special pitch. In the even-numbered innings, the fast ball becomes *four,* with the other pitches moving up one number.

THE ADDITION FACTOR

This should be used in higher levels only. It asks the pitcher to add the number of fingers flashed to determine his pitches, in both two- and three-finger sequences. For instance, in the *two-finger sequence,* the signs could be: *five,* fast ball; *six,* curve; *seven,* slider; *eight,* special pitch. Thus, if the catcher flashes two and three fingers, he wants the fast ball because the total is five. If he flashes four and three, he wants the slider with a seven-finger count. Teams that are experienced and playing at a higher level often utilize a *three-finger* sequence: two fingers, two fingers, one finger equals five, and this means throw the fast ball.

A variation of that theme is the *every-other-digit* count. This is a three-finger flash, with only the first and third signs to be counted. For example, the signs are: *three,* fast ball; *four,* curve; *five,* slider or screwball; and *six,* special pitch. If the catcher flashes 2-2-1, he wants the fast ball since the total of the first and third flashes is three. A 3-2-3 sequence equals six and calls for the special pitch.

ADD-THE-MITT POSITION

Again, to be used only in higher levels of competition. The position of the catcher's mitt on his leg can trigger a starting count number. For example, the mitt at the side of the leg counts as one; over the knee is two; by the bend at the top of the leg is three. Therefore, when the catcher is ready to give the sign, and uses the every-other-digit method with the position of the mitt, the sequence is:

Mitt over the knee, and then flash 2-1-2. The position of the mitt equals two, and the first-and-third-finger flashes equal four. Together they equal six, meaning the catcher wants the special pitch. If he started with his mitt at the side of the leg and then flashed 2-1-1, it totals four and calls for the curve ball.

There even are variations on that theme. The first *or* third finger sign is the one to be counted, together with the mitt position system; or use the middle sign as the only "live" signal, with the other two meaningless. Add the mitt position if you wish.

"Now one run may not seem like much in the first inning but it gets bigger as the game goes on. Later, you could be two down instead of only one. Therefore you have to pass up the chance to sacrifice because you need two runs to tie instead of one. Then by hitting away, you run the risk of hitting into a double play.

"And all because the third base coach didn't use good judgment back there in the first inning."

ADD THE MITT

These systems offer a great number of varieties and are totally interchangeable. But the key to their success is that pitcher and catcher must be certain of what they are calling, and, of course, be able to add correctly. They should discuss the system with each other if possible; and if there is a mixup, then call time out and get it straightened out on the mound. This, of course, tips the opposition that the signals may be changing, but let it figure out which system is being used. Better that than a wild pitch or passed ball that moves the runner along, or worse still, scores a cheap run.

INTENTIONAL PASSES

The *intentional pass* always comes from the coach, who may point to the batter and flash four fingers, then make a motion toward first base, meaning walk him intentionally. Or a coach simply may point to the batter and, knowing the situation with runners on base, the catcher knows there will be an intentional walk.

LOCATING THE BALL

Once the pitcher and catcher agree on their pitches, and how they will signal them, they must concentrate on their location. This is particularly true if the catcher signals that he wants to make a play on a base runner. Any time he flashes that sign, he must get an acknowledgment from the infielder who will take his throw. The pitcher also must know the play is on, and he cannot cross up his catcher by throwing the wrong pitch. To help the catcher, he should throw a fast ball up and away so the catcher will be coming up to get the ball just before it arrives and thus be in a good, strong position to make the throw to the base.

The catcher also must have a sign to wipe off that play if he sees something that tells him it won't work. Again, the rub-off should be acknowledged by the fielder. In this case, the catcher's choice of a pitch will not be dependent upon getting a good throwing position, but rather will be the best possible against the hitter.

All of this applies, too, when the team smells a stolen base and the catcher wants a pitch-out. He will signal the pitcher but the infielders who will cover second or third base also must get the sign and should acknowledge. The pitcher certainly must deliver the ball far enough off the plate where the batter cannot reach it, but where the catcher can be in perfect position to make the throw.

COACHES' QUIZ

1. The most common set of signs for the pitcher is by means of:

   a. flaps
   b. fingers
   c. mask/chest protector/shin guards
   d. none of the above

2. The key to the pitcher signs is:

   a. simplicity
   b. combinations
   c. knowledge of the pitches
   d. none of the above

3. The danger signs for the pitcher with his signs are:

   a. if the catcher is not careful how he gives them
   b. movements of middle infielders
   c. catcher's mannerisms
   d. all of the above

4. Changing signs involves:

   a. the addition factor
   b. the odd-even inning
   c. the add-the-mitt position
   d. all of the above

5. The key to any success in change of sign is:

   a. pitcher and fielders
   b. fielders and catcher
   c. pitcher and catcher
   d. none of the above

6. The most important factor after the choice of pitches is:

   a. location
   b. angle of delivery
   c. position of fielders
   d. all of the above

7. The pitch-out is a move to counteract:

   a. the bunt
   b. the pickoff
   c. the steal
   d. all of the above

CHAPTER 10
HOW TO STEAL SIGNS

As we have seen, the business of transmitting baseball's signs and signals is one of the game's truest art forms. But there also is a flip side to this: stealing them.

That also is an art form, of even a higher magnitude, because of the difficulties involved. Yet every sign and signal is vulnerable because in every opposing dugout there always is a sharpie or two on the lookout for your secrets. That's why I have emphasized the absolute necessity of being so precise and steady in transmitting any kind of sign.

Of course, stealing signs is not limited to just the other dugout. You can—and should—do it because it not only is a part of the game of baseball, it is also one way to get a decided edge on the opponent, particularly one who might be stronger than you.

Basically, such intelligence is the product of experience by managers and coaches who have been giving signs and signals throughout their careers, so they look upon this kind of communication as a second language, easily recognized and understood. The higher the level of competition, the more this applies, so that in the major leagues, there are specialists such as Joe Nossek and, before him, Peanuts Lowery, who were ace decoders and whose service in this specialized field was sought after and handsomely rewarded. In the dugout of every major league team, and those in many of the minor leagues, there always is one person who has a good sense of thievery, perhaps not as keen as Nossek or Lowery, but still good enough so that if the opportunity arises, he'll latch onto the opposition's code.

The deciphering process begins in the dugout and usually involves two or three people: one to watch the coach, one to watch the batter, and, quite often, one to watch the manager. The manager is the one who usually will flash the sign to the coach—in the majors it normally involves only hit-and-run, take, steal, or bunt, though most sacrifice situations are obvious. Quite often to decoy the enemy, though, the manager may have someone

Spy Catchers...

Shortly after the turn of the century when the great Honus Wagner played shortstop for the Pittsburgh Pirates, one of the signals he used when he wanted a throw from the catcher to pick off a runner at second base was to place his glove against his knee.

John McGraw, manager of the New York Giants, stole the sign, and when Wagner did it again, McGraw had his runner break for third base. The player easily made it, and Wagner said nothing.

When the teams played again, Wagner made the same signal, and again the Giants runner broke for third. But this time, the catcher easily threw him out.

McGraw, from the dugout, yelled to Wagner, "You're pretty damned smart for a Dutchman, at that."

One of the favorite vantage points from which to steal a catcher's pitching signs is from the bullpen. Binoculars often are a common piece of equipment in a bullpen, particularly if it affords a "spy" some good cover where he can peer into home plate.

When Al Lopez managed the Chicago White Sox, he had the club purchase a World War II submarine periscope from war surplus and installed it in the Comiskey Park scoreboard in dead center field. He then designated a "skipper" to man the periscope with a direct bead right into the catcher making his

sitting or standing next to him in the dugout do the work while he gives false signals.

If three people are involved in trying to steal the signals, the one watching the manager will concentrate on the upper half of his body because the depth of many dugouts around baseball is such that he usually will give his signs to the coach from the waist up.

Many sign stealers believe it is smarter to concentrate on the opposing manager than on his third base coach because the signs from the dugout are much more simplistic, maybe something as simple as whether he is standing up straight or leaning against a post.

The second person involved will watch the coach and the third looks at the batter as the signs are given. Here, the sharp-eyed spy will catch the clue if the process between coach and batter is not smooth from start to finish. Quite often, the person watching the coach will watch every sign until the man watching the batter says, "Stop!" The last sign he sees before that "stop" often is the one that counts.

How will the man watching the batter know when to say, "Stop!"?

There are a number of keys:

1. The batter may turn his head away as soon as he gets the sign, often unaware that he has done so because it is such a reflex action.

2. The batter may make an unnatural movement of his body or perhaps hitch up his trousers or grip the bat a different way than he usually does—maybe just for a moment, again a reflexive action, but nonetheless a tip-off. If the base runner gets the sign to steal or that a hit-and-run is coming, he may lengthen his lead beyond a point where he normally would stand; or he may look from the coach toward second base; or he might adjust his uniform in an unnatural way. Those are tip-offs.

3. A third base coach may become too deliberate when he gives a sign, slowing down or exaggerating the sign in the course of his body rhythms, and then picking up the tempo once he has flashed the signal. The overemphasis is another tip-off.

4. A strategic move also can be a tip, such as a weak-hitting pitcher coming to bat with men on base and less than two out. Obviously, the pitcher will attempt to sacrifice the runners so the sign stealers will look for the bunt sign, and this can be a key to other strategies such as the squeeze bunt.

5. Often an opposing coach will see a batter hesitate for a moment during the sign giving, and he then will make a mental note of just where the hesitation occurred and after what sign, and then watch what the batter did on the next pitch. All three actions can provide an answer.

To steal signs takes a tremendous amount of concentration to the exclusion of all else in the game. The moment your attention wanders to the events in the game is the moment when the key to breaking a code could be given. That is why managers so often assign coaches to be their "spies" because they have to concentrate on the game as a whole, while the coaches handle specific duties.

The best advice is to keep studying the opposing dugout, the coach, the batter, and base runners, and sooner or later a pattern may emerge.

Of course, the question arises: What do I do if I believe my signs have been stolen?

First, you should be sure, and the tip-offs should usually come on plays like stolen bases when runners are thrown out after pitch-outs or by defensive plays by infielders who totally ignore the action of the batter. The quick remedy is to change the indicator sign, and go from there. It is quite difficult to change an entire package in mid-game, though some will revert to a "touch system," where they institute a certain number of touches to an area to indicate what the sign will be. Pitchers and catchers, who are forever changing signs because of base runners at second base peering into home plate, do the switches automatically.

And the better question is: How do I avoid having my signs stolen?

First, be certain that your batters and base runners look through the entire sequence. You must emphasize in your drills—and even make a part of your drills—this action, to the point where each man is acutely aware that he must do nothing out of the ordinary to tip off what sign he has received.

Second, with younger players, have a release sign and insist that the youngster look at the coach until that sign has been given. The young player should even be instructed to look past the release sign so that this signal is not tipped, and to get into the habit of being very natural while getting a sign.

Remember, baseball's signs and signals are a very special language that only you want translated to your team's benefit. And if that language is utilized properly, it will be clearly understood and used to the greatest advantage—to winning and to the success of your team.

signs and relay the information by phone to the dugout.

The man who is credited with starting the sign-stealing business was an outfielder named Dan Murphy, who couldn't make it with the Philadelphia A's three quarters of a century ago, but who was a born sign stealer. A's manager Connie Mack installed him on a rooftop across the street from the A's ball park and gave him a pair of binoculars.

Within two innings, he could decode the catcher's signals and flashed the upcoming pitches either by crossed-arm signals or by twirling a weather vane in opposite directions, according to fast ball or curve.

But one day, his vane went out of control during a violent wind storm...and so, for a time, did the A's signal stealing.

COACHES' QUIZ

1. The deciphering of signs and signals begins in:

   a. the clubhouse
   b. the coaching box
   c. the dugout
   d. all of the above

2. Many sign stealers believe the one to watch is the:

   a. manager
   b. third base coach
   c. first base coach
   d. pitching coach

3. To steal signs takes great:

   a. luck
   b. knowledge
   c. concentration
   d. none of the above

4. Usually the first sign changed if the opposition steals your sign is:

   a. the bunt
   b. the hit-and-run
   c. the indicator
   d. none of the above

ANSWERS TO COACHES' QUIZZES

Chapter 1 (Baseball Signs)
       1. d.; 2. a.; 3. a; 4. d.; 5. a.; 6. c.; 7. c.; 8. a.; 9. c.

Chapter 2 (Bunt Sign)
       1. a.; 2. b.; 3. a.; 4. c.; 5. c.; 6. a.; 7. a.; 8. b.

Chapter 3 (Hit and Run/Run and Hit)
       1. b.; 2. a.; 3. c.; 4. c.; 5. c.; 6. d.; 7. b.

Chapter 4 (Take or Hit Away)
       1. c.; 2. c.; 3. a.; 4. c.

Chapter 5 (Stealing Second and Third)
       1. d.; 2. b.; 3. d.; 4. a.; 5. c.

Chapter 6 (Slide or Stand Up)
       1. c.; 2. c.; 3. d.; 4. d.; 5. a.; 6. a.

Chapter 7 (Infield/Outfield Signals)
       1. a.; 2. c.; 3. b.; 4. b.; 5. c.; 6. b.; 7. c.; 8. c.; 9. b.; 10. a.

Chapter 8 (Infield Pickoffs and Double Steals)
       1. b.; 2. d.; 3. a.; 4. c.; 5. b.; 6. b.; 7. b.; 8. a.

Chapter 9 (Pitching Signs)
       1. b.; 2. a.; 3. d.; 4. d.; 5. c.; 6. a.; 7. c.

Chapter 10 (How to Steal Signs)
       1. c.; 2. a.; 3. c.; 4. c.

INDEX

ABOUT THE AUTHORS

TOM PETROFF

Veteran baseball coach Tom Petroff is currently an assistant coach at the University of Iowa. A former pro baseball player, he was recently inducted into the NCAA Coaches Hall of Fame. Petroff was the College Division Coach of the Year in 1972 while head coach at the University of Northern Colorado, he coached the U.S. Amateur Team at the World Games in Seoul, Korea (1982) and at the World Friendship Series in Newark, Ohio (1981) and was elected President of the American Baseball Coaches Association in 1984. He is renowned for his teaching skills and has conducted more than 60 clinics across the country during his long and distinguished career.

JACK CLARY

Freelance writer Jack Clary has co-authored, written and edited nearly two dozen books during some 30 years as a journalist. These include the *1986 Pro Football Scouting Report; PB,* the autobiography of Paul Brown; *The Art of Quarterbacking* with Cincinnati Bengals' quarterback Ken Anderson; *Pro Football's Great Moments; Jim Palmer's Way to Fitness* with the former Baltimore Orioles' pitcher; *Careers in Sport;* and *The Gamemakers* with such successful NFL coaches as Don Shula, Tom Landry, Chuck Noll, Bum Phillips, John Madden and Chuck Knox. In addition to working as a consultant in all aspects of sports journalism and marketing for his firm, Sports Media Enterprises, Clary spent 17 years as a sportswriter and columnist for the Associated Press, *New York World Telegram & Sun* and the *Boston Herald Traveler.*